Living in the Eternal

A STUDY OF GEORGE SANTAYANA

Photograph taken from the dust jacket of *The Idea of Christ in the Gospels* (Charles Scribner's Sons, 1946). Used by permission.

Living in the Eternal

A STUDY OF GEORGE SANTAYANA

Anthony Woodward

VANDERBILT UNIVERSITY PRESS
Nashville, Tennessee
1988

For the privilege of being allowed to study rare unpublished material by Santayana, the author wishes to thank the Houghton Library at Harvard University and the Butler Library at Columbia University, New York.

The author and publisher make grateful acknowledgement to the publishers of the following books and periodicals for permission to reprint passages in this collection that first appeared in their publications:

George Braziller, Inc. For passages reprinted from *Santayana: The Later Years* by Daniel Cory by permission of George Braziller, Inc., New York. Copyright 1963.

Constable Publishers. For permission to reprint passages from the following works by George Santayana: *Soliloquies in England* (1922), *Dialogues in Limbo* (1923), *Scepticism and Animal Faith* (1923), *Obiter Scripta* (1936), *Dominations and Powers* (1951), and *The Letters of George Santayana*, ed. Daniel Cory (1955).

Margot Cory. For permission to reprint in the United States and Canada passages from the works by George Santayana listed above.

Duke University Press. Anthony Woodward, "The Solitude of Santayana," in *South Atlantic Quarterly* 86: 2, pp. 110-122. Copyright © 1987 Duke University Press.

Faber and Faber Limited. Sixteen lines from "To An Old Philosopher in Rome." Reprinted by permission of Faber and Faber Ltd from THE COLLECTED POEMS OF WALLACE STEVENS.

Farrar, Straus & Giroux, Inc. Excerpts from EUROPE WITHOUT BAEDEKER by Edmund Wilson. Copyright © 1946, 1966 by Edmund Wilson. Reprinted by permission of Farrar Straus & Giroux, Inc.

Alfred A. Knopf, Inc. Sixteen lines from "To An Old Philosopher in Rome." Copyright 1952 by Wallace Stevens. Reprinted from THE COLLECTED POEMS OF WALLACE STEVENS by Wallace Stevens, by permission of Alfred A. Knopf, Inc.

The Ohio University Press. *Athens and Jerusalem* by Lev Shestov. Copyright 1966. Reprinted with the permission of The Ohio University Press, Athens.

Library of Congress Cataloging-in-Publication Data

Woodward, Anthony.
  Living in the eternal.

  Bibliography: p.
  Includes index.
  1. Santayana, George, 1863-1952. I. Title.
B945.S24W66 1988   191   87-23022
ISBN 0-8265-1227-5

To Caro and Nicholas

Dates of Publication of
Principal Writings of Santayana

Contents

Preface

The body of Santayana's writing has for too long been recalled as a monument of serene humanism, on the basis of *The Life of Reason* and some early essays. His later work was founded on scepticism, materialism, and ambiguously mitigated irrationalism. Yet he did not convey his outlook in any disintegrating mode of twentieth-century anguish, as it might have seemed to warrant. Instead he annexed in imagination the spiritual transcendence of time and history found in many religious philosophies of East and West, and sustained in the modern world the role of detached contemplative and sage. To this role he brought a masterful intellect, wit, candour, and unassailable elevation. He wrought "a style from a despair," but the style does not abandon us to despair.

Santayana has suffered unmerited neglect. Perhaps worse than neglect: the hole-in-corner fame of being tellingly quoted in other men's writings, but with few in recent decades caring to come to terms with the distinguished source of the quotations.

Anthony Woodward

· 1 ·

"I live in the Eternal"

ON August 7, 1944, shortly after the arrival of the Allied armies in Rome near the end of the Second World War, *Life* magazine published a photograph of the eighty-year-old Santayana, holding some reading-matter in his hand and sitting on a park bench. The picture was accompanied by a caption and some further comments. The smile of the sage was equable, his demeanour discreetly jaunty. The caption read, "George Santayana tears eight pages out of a book for his afternoon reading in a Roman park. When he has read them he throws them away." The story is apocryphal[1] and makes Santayana seem rather silly if it is taken as a literal account of his habits. Yet like many a good myth it has symbolic truth and catches a certain airy dismissiveness in the mask he sometimes chose to present to the world. The prurient fascination that this spectacle evoked in the journalist is evident from the tone of the other comments, which conclude: "Of communism and fascism he said: 'doubtless there are good things in both.' Of war he knew nothing. Said he: 'I live in the Eternal.'"

To "live in the Eternal" was for Santayana to live in what he called the realm of Essence, a traditional term he used when constructing a sceptical philosophy of detachment from existence. Existence he once described, with his usual happy gift of phrase, as "normal madness." Essences are the formal characteristics of things: what they are, as distinct from the fact that they exist. The notion is scholastic in origin. With Santayana it was more an attitude toward life than a cogent logical doctrine, and the interweaving of imagination with reasoning in his philosophy is its prime fascination as well as its drawback.

1

Timothy Sprigge, who has written a good technical account of Santayana's work, is led to remark with a touch of desperation at one point in his discussion of Santayana's elusive doctrine of essence that it means "savouring the character of certain forms of being, this colour, this pattern, this idea."[2] That catches the right mood, I think. Santayana himself writes that it is a "trick of arresting the immediate that is in one sense an interruption to life; it is proper only to poets, mystics or epicureans." He adds that it is incompatible with "a political, censorious temper."[3] There also is a helpful hint. Let us now hear Santayana at slightly greater length on this topic, in a passage that characteristically blends emotion with exposition. He is discussing Proust, whose intuitions in this realm he found congenial:

An essence is simply the recognisable character of any object or feeling, all of it that can actually be possessed in sensation or recovered in memory, or transcribed in art, or conveyed to another mind. . . . The hopeless flux and the temporal order of things are not ultimately interesting: they belong merely to the material occasions on which essences occur, or to the flutterings of attention, hovering like a moth about lights which are eternal.[4]

Ascent to that sphere of spiritual freedom and light comes when all the energies of the soul focus with undistracted intuition upon some pure essence, whether it be "a breath of morning air or the sum total of possible knowledge."[5]

The sum total of possible knowledge would normally be taken to describe the content of the mind of God. God, who by His nature "lives in the Eternal," knows and loves all things in their ordained imperfections and their varied strivings after the good. Santayana believed that the truly philosophical spirit, too, might in some analogous fashion transcend its human egotism and aspire to "understand things as they are in themselves and to love in them the good they love."[6] Such a disposition is encompassed by the theological virtue of charity, and Santayana's greatest book, *The Realm of Spirit,* culminates in a vision of existence that has an aura both Christian and Catholic. But it is a Catholic vision informed by the ideal of perfect illumination, and never surrenders itself to the dark enterprise of faith. There was nothing of the "infant crying in the night" about Santayana. He tried to be godlike; he did not abandon himself to God. He reminds us a little, perhaps, of some Gnostic Christian of Alexandria in the early centuries of the faith, for whom love has been swallowed up in knowledge and the believer consummated in the sage. A bitter-sweet knowingness that gazes down on all things and comprehends them with suave tolerance was the characteristic pose of Santayana in his later years. The arrival of the Allied army in Rome, at the end of the Second World War, along with its accompanying journalists, did not much dent this *ataraxia*.

The image of ascent to a rewarding vantage point, where the mind may repose and survey the accidents of existence, is fundamental to Santayana's outlook:

> Life, if by the word we understand the process of mutation, is itself death; to be fed is to kill, to advance is to reject and abandon. The truly creative moment is only upward, and life, in so far as it means light and accomplishment, is only some predestined intuition achieved, some wished for essence made manifest.[7]

Lionel Trilling picked on that feature of surveying existence from an inner spiritual zenith as a refreshing antidote to overexposure to current trends: "This is a nearly forgotten possibility of the mind; it is not approved by the hidden prepotent Censor of modern modes of thought. To look within is permitted; to look around is encouraged; but best not look down—not realistic, not engaged, not democratic."[8]

Platonic and Catholic traditions employ such vertical images of transcendence, and Santayana was near to both, but he endeavoured to transpose their outlook to a naturalistic plane. The region whence spirit arises to the contemplation of eternal essences he called the Realm of Matter. It alone exists. We interpret matter more or less successfully with the aid of units of meaning called "essences," but matter in its own dynamic nature is obscure to us. We know it by "animal faith." Whenever our animal being gives us pause from the automatism of action we may dwell on such essences as are congenial to our nature, each essence being eternal in its own realm, but available for contemplation whenever the spiritual energies of the human organism are fortunately disposed. To live thus is to live in the eternal. It is to live in the mind:

> To substitute the society of ideas for that of things is simply to live in the mind; it is to survey the world of existence in its truth and beauty rather than in its personal perspectives, or with practical urgency. It is the sole path to happiness for the intellectual man, because the intellectual man cannot be satisfied with a world of perpetual change, defeat and imperfection. It is the path trodden by ancient philosophers and modern saints or poets; not, of course, by modern writers on philosophy (except Spinoza), because these have not been philosophers in the vital sense: they have practised no spiritual discipline, suffered no change of heart, but lived on exactly like other professors.[9]

In a chastened moment Santayana once reflected on the possibility that his Realm of Essence might be, as Bertrand Russell had said, "a monk's dream." Nevertheless it helped him to construct a philosophical system that was not so much an explanatory hypothesis as a way of liberation for the solitary spirit, akin in many respects to what is found in the philosophical disciplines of the East. He never ceased to be a monk of the intellect, though admittedly, in his years of maturity, a rather well-heeled one. An upper-storey suite in Rome's Hotel Bristol, or a congenial room at the Danieli, is a Thebaid many of us would be prepared to contemplate. Daniel Cory, the secretary and friend of the philosopher's Italian years, from the early 1920s until his death in 1952, gives us this glimpse of him in 1935 at the Hotel Bristol, at the end of a day of writing, of walking and reading on the Pincio, concluding with a chat on philosophical topics with Cory before dinner:

> In my mind's eye I can see him walk over to the large front window that opened on the Piazza Barberini and gaze for a few moments up the lighted Via Tritone before drawing the curtains for the night. Santayana liked that view from his top-storey window; it was gay and yet sufficiently distant to be undisturbing.[10]

The gay yet undisturbing spectacle Santayana surveyed was of course the Fascist Rome of Mussolini in the mid-1930s. Fascism and Communism, however flawed in practice and different in emphasis, both derive from an intuited ideal of possible harmony between the individual and the social whole, and in that ideal sense there were "doubtless . . . good things in both," as Santayana told the disconcerted journalist of *Life* magazine. Even in practice Santayana was often prepared to put in a good word for aspects of Mussolini's Italy, where he lived for a fair number of contented years. To a former colleague in America he once wrote,

> Another true satisfaction to me is the new régime in Italy and Spain, American in its futurism and its confident hopes, but classical in its reliance on discipline and its love of a beautiful finitude and decision. That dreadful loose dream of liberalism seems to be fading away at last. Poor England and France are paying the penalty for having drugged themselves so thoroughly with that verbal poison.[11]

That was in 1926. Nine years later, when the Abyssinian crisis was brewing, he wrote from Rome to another American friend:

> Naturally, we are living under a war-cloud; but I hope it won't burst. My sympathies are anti-English now; gradually since the war all my Anglomania has faded away. The British bully is traditional, the English prig is familiar; but the two were never before so well combined as in Mr. Eden. I prefer the Bolshies; and perhaps everywhere, through one approach or another, it is to State Socialism we are bound.[12]

He liked to tease his American capitalist friends and relatives of the interwar years with occasional disobliging references to the rootlessness of the capitalist system, and to dwell calmly on the interest of the Soviet experiment. We may infer that Santayana's remark to the *Life* magazine journalist was also a teasing one. He was a master of the put-down. "Aloofness and facile contempt were his defects," Bertrand Russell once remarked.[13]

The limitations of Santayana's temperament are tempting game for anyone wishing to relate his thought to his character. Thus far, he may well sound spectral and alienating. According to many observers he was nothing of the kind: we hear of his radiant charm, his unassuming distinction of manner, the glowing intensity of his eyes, his utterly transforming and delightful smile, his kindliness. Nevertheless William James, his teacher and then his colleague at Harvard around the turn of the century, who admired his intellectual powers, remarked of him that he had "put his heart on ice"; and in a posthumously published letter James referred to Santayana's principal early work, *The*

Life of Reason, as the "perfection of rottenness in a philosophy."[14] "Moribund latinity" was another of his choice dismissals. One wonders what he would have thought if he had lived to read Santayana's mature philosophical synthesis, *Realms of Being,* with its contemplative aestheticism and its Olympian detachment from the volatile currents of existence to which William James was so attached. *The Life of Reason* was a good deal more moralistic and progressive, closer in fact to the meliorism of James himself, and for that reason Santayana later came to dislike it.

William James gave utterance to other opinions of Santayana, more temperate and fair, even enthusiastic. Santayana in turn paid James a noble tribute at the end of his essay on him in *Character and Opinion in the United States,* and also learned much from James's teaching on the flux of experience, which he later put to use in his own accounts of the radical contingency of existence. Yet there was a fundamental antipathy, as Santayana later confessed to Cory: he "didn't like him personally."[15] Perhaps this is the moment to see how James looked from the perspective of Santayana's temperament:

William James shared the passions of liberalism. He belonged to the left, which, as they say in Spain, is the side of the heart, as the right is that of the liver; at any rate there was much blood and no gall in his philosophy. He was one of those elder Americans still disquieted by the ghost of tyranny, social and ecclesiastical. Even the beauties of the past troubled him; he had a puritan feeling that they were tainted. . . . There is a sense in which James was not a philosopher at all. He once said to me: "What a curse philosophy would be if we couldn't forget all about it!" In other words, philosophy was not to him what it has been to so many, a consolation and sanctuary in a life which would have been unsatisfying without it. It would be incongruous, therefore, to expect of him that he should build a philosophy like an edifice to go and live in for good.[16]

Two things there must give us pause: the reference to Spain, and the view of philosophy as a consolation and a sanctuary.

Santayana never ceased in some paradoxical manner to be a traditional Spanish Catholic in outlook, even though he never practised his religion after an early age, and his main significant contacts with Spain, after leaving it as a child, took the form of extended visits to see his half-sister, Susana, perhaps the greatest single personal influence on his life. In traditional Spanish Catholicism scorn of the world is fundamental, especially when worldliness is bound up with a busy democratic meliorism that looks in the currents of earthly history for some progressive realisation of ideal good. All such is *Nada:* Nothing. When literal belief in a supernatural realm where the ideal good is laid up fails, as happened to Santayana, the spirit turns inward and constructs for itself a haven in which to pursue its missed vocation, which becomes "precisely dominion, spiritual dominion, without distraction, responsibility or power."[17] With such phrasing Santayana gave provocative form to an ideal with some august antecedents:

> *Socrates:* The wise man in public and private life will put aside all that might overturn the constitution of his soul.
> *Glaucon:* . . . He will take a part, you are saying, in the state we have been founding: a state whose being is in ideas only, for I do not believe it can have any existence on earth.
> *Socrates:* Well, maybe its pattern is already there in heaven for him to see who so desires it; and seeing it, he makes himself its citizen. And the question of its present or future existence makes no difference. He who sees it will live by its laws and no other.[18]

> The pursuit of (philosophic wisdom) is thought to offer pleasures marvellous for their purity and their enduringness, and it is to be expected that those who know will pass their time more pleasantly than those who enquire. And the self-sufficiency that is spoken of must belong most to the contemplative activity.[19]

One must immediately qualify the effect of such passages from Plato and Aristotle by a reminder that both their doctrines took account of links between the contemplative and the active modes of life. Yet the ideal of individual self-sufficiency in Plato and Aristotle prefigured something increasingly widespread among philosophers in the later stages of Hellenism, both in the Greek world after Alexander the Great had destroyed the autonomy of the city-states and in the Roman Empire. Werner Jaeger wrote, in terms that remind one vividly of Santayana's remark on his own philosophical ideal contrasted with that of William

James: "The philosophical systems of the Hellenistic Age were for their followers a sort of spiritual shelter."[20]

Three such systems come to mind, each having a bearing on Santayana taken as Hellenistic sage redivivus in the modern world: Stoicism, Epicureanism, and Pyrrhonism, especially the latter two.

For Santayana, the atomism of Epicurus and Lucretius would not have been a literal belief, but he was thoroughly at home with the notion that the ultimate determinant of all things must be a substance physical in nature. Its essence—and here lies the Pyrrhonist in Santayana—we cannot know. Pyrrho was totally sceptical of all reports on the nature of being; they are at best mental constructions, figments. Santayana, too, was convinced that our mental reports on existence are all imaginative in kind, though many are efficacious in practice: a phosphorescent play of ideas on a sea of unknown origins and dimension. The Stoics, by contrast, upheld a belief in the existence of an intrinsically rational world-order of which human reason is a part. Such a cosmology was alien to Santayana's view that existence is an irrational flux where little eddies of rational order occasionally take shape. Yet the spiritual attitude of Santayana has distinct Stoic qualities, if one makes allowance for the intrinsic frailty of spirit in his irrationalist materialism; and that spiritual attitude is one A. J. Festugière held to be common to Stoicism, Epicureanism, and Pyrrhonism.[21] It is, disregarding their doctrinal differences, an attitude of detachment, indifference, and superiority to fortune.

The belief in fortune, fate, and chance as the cardinal powers of existence became commonplace in the world of late pagan antiquity; thence it was but a step to the attitude of the Gnostics, who saw existence as in thrall to irrational demonic forces that they identified with matter; it became the goal of the illuminated being to find release from matter in a higher and purer realm of spirit. It has occasionally struck me that in Santayana's *Realms of Being* we have something like a de-mythologised latter-day Gnosticism (a point to consider in a later chapter). Plotinus, admittedly no friend to the Gnostics, epitomises the attitude of mind we are considering in a passage such as the following:

For everything that looks to another is under spell to that: what we look to, draws us magically. Only the self-intent go free of magic. Hence every action has magic as its source, and the entire life of the practical man is a bewitchment: we move to that only which has wrought a fascination upon us. . . . Contemplation alone stands untouched by magic: no man self-gathered falls to a spell: for he is one, and that unity is all he perceives, so that his reason is not beguiled but holds the due course, fashioning its own career and accomplishing its task.[22]

Santayana was very much what Plotinus calls there a "self-gathered" man: a nice phrase for the detachment from chance and change sought by wise men in Hellenistic antiquity, with which Santayana confessed to feeling a kinship. Partly this was a matter of temperament. Partly it must have been due to factors in late nineteenth-century civilisation that gave a renewed resonance to the Hellenistic fascination with chance and change: the Darwinian emphasis on the element of chance in the evolutionary process, and the waste and carnage entailed in that evolution; irrationalist currents, especially the notion of Will in Schopenhauer, a major influence on Santayana; the theory of indeterminism in Lotze, on whom Santayana wrote his doctoral thesis; the critical speculation among physicists about natural law, and the increasing stress on chance and probability; and the mistrust of rationalist systems of the universe, which Santayana would have imbibed from William James but which elicited in him a fundamentally different response. For James, the radical contingency of existence was a challenge and an opportunity. For Santayana, it was a predicament. It drove him to the posture of spiritual detachment whose analogies in Hellenistic antiquity have been seen. It also evoked in him, at least as early as the 1890s, an interest in similar qualities of Oriental speculation. That, along with the element of Gnosticism, will have to be considered. At this point, however, it seems fitting to explore a little further Santayana's link with an aspect of late nineteenth-century culture in the Western world.

Walter Pater, in his essay on Winckelmann in *The Renaissance*, sums up thus the impression made on him by the Panathenaic frieze of youths on horseback from the Acropolis, now in the

British Museum: "This purity of life . . . pregnant with the possibilities of a whole world closed within it, is the highest expression of the indifference which lies beyond the relative or partial."[23] Pater, impresario of the cultivated sensation, here reveals the tilt toward inhumanity that goes with the aesthetic attitude. Like many aesthetes of the later nineteenth century, he never ceased to accord the classical period of Greek civilisation a special reverence, although this was inconsistent with the relativism implied by his philosophy of sensation. In that sentence on the Panathenaic frieze he significantly picks on the Apollonian qualities of impartiality and indifference as having a special aesthetic vibrancy. Santayana, too, can in one light be considered just such another Hellenising aesthete of the late nineteenth century, even though he outgrew his attachment to things Greek as touchstones of perfection after the publication of *The Life of Reason* in the early 1900s. He nevertheless remained the hierophant of perfected form even in the much more harsh and Heraclitean setting of his later *Realms of Being,* whose crowning spiritual doctrine of an impartial love of all things for the diverse perfections toward which they strive can sound, to an unfriendly critic, like the rarefied indifference of an aesthete.

Such an imputation of aestheticism would not have been acceptable to Santayana himself, except in the most carefully qualified terms. Overtly he disliked aestheticism, doubtless in part because he associated it with the messy life of someone like Lionel Johnson, whom he had known quite well as a young Harvard man visiting England in the 1890s. Yet Lionel Johnson addressed a poem to him; and Santayana's own attitude was by no means unsympathetic. Indeed in a letter of 1928, written to a young man who had sent him a book on the "scientific method" in aesthetics, he wrote,

You must remember that we were not very much later than Ruskin, Pater, Swinburne, and Matthew Arnold: our atmosphere was that of poets and persons touched with religious enthusiasm or religious sadness. Beauty (which must'nt be mentioned now) was then a living presence, or an aching absence, day and night: history was always singing in our ears; and not even psychology or the analysis of works of art could take away from art its human implications. It was the great memorial to us, the great revelation, of what the soul had lived on, and had lived with, in her better days.[24]

In a passage like that, Santayana is casting his net widely. It is no precious formalism that he is identifying with the aesthetic phase of the late nineteenth century in which his young manhood was passed. He is commending love of beauty as the poignant and intense culmination of the human capacity for experience. "In art more directly than in other activities man's self-expression is cumulative and finds an immediate reward." That sentence comes from Santayana's *The Life of Reason* and not, as one could have suspected, from one of Oscar Wilde's essays.

Even in the odd casual remark Santayana struck at times a Wildean note that gave another slant to the link with aestheticism. When he was already a middle-aged professor at Harvard, he wrote to a congenial young friend that he might "go back to Heidelberg—it is the only place in Germany that tempts me back—to an international philosophic congress that is to meet there. I should see in the flesh a lot of ugly old men whose names I have seen in print all my life."[25] It is perhaps worth remarking at this point that Santayana's preferences ran to young men who were handsome. Did he actively indulge these preferences? Little, if at all, one would guess. Sexually, he appears to have been somewhat uninvolved. He certainly liked, however, to live his social life at Harvard mainly among senior students of the more gentlemanly kind. In C. M. Flandrau's *Harvard Episodes* (1897) the figure of Mr. Thorn is supposed to be a skit on Santayana: Thorn, in his reputed over-fondness for gilded youth, gives a good mark to a student's essay that he has not read. The author comments, "Youth, energy and cleanliness were the trinity Thorn worshipped." In later years, when Santayana had resigned his post at Harvard and settled in Rome, he told Cory that various people at Harvard "must have suspected something unusual in his make-up"; that he "felt acutely at times their silent disapproval"; and that it was one of the things that made him determined to retire from teaching.[26] The homosexual don who restricts his activities to the odd playful punch or squeeze was not an unusual figure in superior academic circles of an older generation. That, however, was not Santayana's style. It seems doubtful, from what he told Cory on the same occasion, whether he even quite realised in his earlier years the ambiguity of his sexual nature. In any case that nature was never very intense. ("Love has never made me long unhappy, nor sexual impulse uncomfortable.")[27] In speaking of Housman, he added to Cory, "I suppose he was what people nowadays call homosexual. . . . I think I must have been that in my Harvard days—although I was unconscious of it at the time."[28]

Santayana's summing up of his Harvard years in his autobiography hints only in the most oblique fashion at the perturbations just touched on, in the course of a paragraph of typically crisp detachment:

> When I resigned my professorship my name had figured in the Harvard Catalogue, in one capacity or another, for thirty years. Yet that long career had been slow and insecure, made in an atmosphere of mingled favour and distrust. My relations with President Eliot and with other influential persons had always been strained. I had disregarded or defied public opinion by not becoming a specialist, but writing pessimistic, old-fashioned verses, continuing to range superficially over literature and philosophy, being indiscernibly a Catholic or an atheist, attacking Robert Browning, prophet of the half-educated and half-believing, avoiding administrative duties, neglecting the intelligentsia, frequenting the society of undergraduates and fashionable ladies, spending my holidays abroad, and even appearing as a witness in the disreputable Russell trial. At the same time, in private, I had breathed the pleasantest airs of sympathy and friendship. My philosophic colleagues had supported me, my old friends had been faithful, appreciative, and always hospitable, my new friends had multiplied in numbers and influence, my books, though received coldly at first, had attained a certain reputation. I was still disliked, but I was swallowed.[29]

The latter sentences of the passage are smoothly conciliatory in the public manner of his autobiography, where he never lets his guard down for a moment. In letters he was more candid. In 1911, just prior to his resignation, he wrote from Harvard to his sister in Spain:

> When I am here in the midst of the dull round, a sort of instinct of courtesy makes me take it for granted, and I become almost uncon-

scious of how much I hate it all: otherwise I couldn't have stood it *for forty years!* . . . I am very sick of America and of professors and professoresses, and I am pining for a sunny, quiet, remote, friendly, intellectual, obscure existence, with large horizons and no empty noise in the foreground.[30]

In later life he told Robert Lowell, when referring to his Harvard years, that "my times and my surroundings were deadly for my vocation."[31] Philosophy for him was a consecrated and clarified way of life, not a professional occupation to be certified by a requisite number of man-hours and publications. The Harvard of President Eliot—already putting Ph.D. specialisation at a premium in the humanities, increasingly alert to sheer numbers—struck both William James and Santayana as showing a strain of philistinism.

Santayana resigned his Chair at the age of forty-nine in 1912, when his mother died and he came into some money. The money was skilfully managed for him by his Boston Sturgis relatives (his mother's first marriage had been to a Sturgis), and the comparative affluence he enjoyed until the Second World War must have facilitated his detachment and made possible his staying at expensive hotels on the continent of Europe. After the Great War, he gradually made Rome his principal base. When not living in hotels, Santayana sometimes shared a flat in Paris or a villa in Italy with C. A. Strong, a millionaire philosopher-friend from student days who had married a Rockefeller daughter. Occasionally they squabbled about Cory's secretarial services. Santayana was quite hurt by Strong's brusque ways.

It was an odd life, viewed from outside, with an element of unconscious pathos: homeless, itinerant from one grand hotel to another, writing long, marvellous letters in which he gave all of his mind and nothing of himself, increasingly doting on Cory in harmless avuncular fashion. It was the life of a man all of whose energies fed a single flame of thought and contemplation. The whole second part of his life must seem an offence to energetic altruists, although Epicurus might have understood him. In later years he grew into the role of gracious yet reclusive sage so clearly intended for him by nature. Earlier his isolation and aloofness had a provocatively flippant edge. Bertrand Russell gives us this glimpse of Santayana in England at Cambridge, in 1915:

He was suave, meticulous in his ways, and very seldom excited. A few days before the Battle of the Marne, when the capture of Paris by the Germans seemed imminent, he remarked to me, 'I think I must go to Paris, because my winter underclothes are there, and I should not like the Germans to get them. I have also left there the manuscript of a book on which I have been working for the last ten years; but I don't mind so much about that.' However the Battle of the Marne obviated the necessity of his journey.

One evening in Cambridge, after I had been seeing him every day for some time, he remarked to me, 'I am going to Seville tomorrow. I wish to be in a place where people do not restrain their passions.'[32]

That is the attitudinising of a dandy. Yet the airy provocations of the dandy can be a legitimate weapon for curbing pretensions to false seriousness. It becomes a duty to disconcert the worldly, the optimistic, the self-important. Santayana throughout all his writings never entirely lost that air of a man of the 1890s who had read his Schopenhauer. In the first volume of his auto-biography he describes his youth in Boston after his mother had brought him there from Spain. The jolt comes in the first sentence. Its substance is qualified, but not withdrawn:

That the real was rotten and only the imaginary at all interesting seemed to me axiomatic. That was too sweeping; yet allowing for the rash generalizations of youth, it is still what I think. My philosophy has never changed. It is by no means an artificial academic hypothesis; it doesn't appeal at all to the professors; it is a system of presuppositions and categories discovered already alive and at work within me, willy-nilly, like existence itself, and virtually present not only in the boy but in the embryo.

I say "within me", because there I have finally deciphered it by analysis; but it was not peculiar to me. It was common then in certain circles and was called pessimism. Pessimism is an accidental moralistic name for it; because the philosophy in question is a system of cosmology, a view of nature and history; moral preferences or judgments are not central in it.[33]

Take the quietly calculated diabolism of this section from the second volume of the autobiography:

Man was not made to understand the world, but to live in it. Yet nature, in some of us, lets out her secret; it spoils the game, but it associates us with her own impartiality. We cannot abdicate that privilege. It is final, ultimate, proper for the funeral oration over the earth: but those who are destined to live in this world had better not hear of it, or if they hear of it had better not take it too much to heart.[34]

And this, also from *The Middle Span,* concerning Santayana's friend, the young Harvard poet Trumbull Stickney:

I think he distrusted me also for being a materialist, not so much in theory, for we never discussed that, but in my constant sense of the animal basis of spirit, and my disrespect for any claim on the part of spirit to govern the world. He feared me. I was a Mephistopheles masquerading as a conservative. I defended the past because once it had been victorious and had brought something beautiful to light; but I had no clear expectation of better things in the future. He saw looming behind me the dreadful spectres of truth and death.[35]

The next two sentences come from *The Realm of Spirit,* the crowning volume of *Realms of Being:* "We talk of 'life' as if it were unquestionably something precious or divine. Perhaps a part of the vocation of spirit may be to overcome this preju-dice."[36] Finally, most revealing of all, consider these sentences from the "General Confession," which Santayana wrote for a collection of essays on his work published in 1940. Once again he reflects on his youthful self in the later nineteenth century:

I was delighted with anything, like Mallock's *Is Life Worth Living?* which seemed to rebuke the fatuity of that age. For my own part, I was quite sure that life was not worth living; for if religion was false everything was worthless, and almost everything, if religion was true. In this youthful pessimism I was hardly more foolish than so many amateur medievalists and religious aesthetes of my generation. I saw the same alternative between Catholicism and complete disillusion; but I was never afraid of disillusion and I have chosen it.[37]

"I have chosen it." Such calm finality retains the kernel of early aesthetic pessimism but gives it the ring of a matured judgement.

The pessimism lasted. But so did the aestheticism. Whenever one finds oneself in difficulties with Santayana's doctrine of spirit and its redemption through the intuition of essence, it is helpful to remember the following brief passage from his autobiography, written in old age. The experience of beauty re-mained for him the most vivid, though by no means the unique, instance of what it meant to retain contemplation as the culminating factor of existence. He watched a young friend gaze enraptured at a painting:

And when Bob Potter, so very tall and thin, so refined and so embarrassed, said *pfui!* or when he was religiously silent and evidently moved in the presence of something exquisite, my own load was lifted, and I saw how instrumental were all the labour and history of man, to be crowned, if crowned at all, only in intuition.[38]

In the same section of his autobiography Santayana remarked that the pure intuitive appreciation of Bob Potter taught him more about art than the knowledgeable sophistication of Charles Loeser, a wealthy friend closely connected with the Berenson circle in Italy. Santayana also moved in that circle at times, and it is an indication of how cautious we should be in aligning him too closely with aestheticism that he largely disapproved of it, and later became estranged from Berenson. Santayana wanted art to flower naturally from a whole civilised social context, and not just be a hothouse bloom in lifeless galleries or in the mansions of millionaires. One could argue that this made Santayana a more thoroughgoing aesthete; alternatively, that the narrower, historical connotations of aestheticism are limiting when trying to understand him.

"The other day, awaking from absorption in the newspaper, whom should I see before me but Berenson!" Santayana wrote to a friend from the Hotel Danieli in 1939. "He surprised me by talking with juvenile enthusiasm about 'art' (as if we were still in the 1890s)."[39] Berenson in turn wrote about the same meeting to Judge Learned Hand. He had told Santayana that he was in Venice to look at pictures. The latter remarked, "Oh, I thought they had done all they could to advance you along the line of your ambitions." Berenson was by this stage of his life as well cocooned as any man has ever been against people making that kind of remark to him, and one feels an unworthy reflex of enjoyment that Santayana made it. The claws of the two polished elderly Olympians were sharp. Berenson concluded, "All in all he left me the impression of a very self-satisfied, rather maliciously cynical, sniggering, sneering old man. He has no wife nor child, nor friend nor foe, no needs except the elementary ones, and yet is happy, consciously happy."[40] With dismissive candour Santayana in turn finished off Berenson:

> How little sympathy there is at bottom between people who don't like each other but like the same 'subjects', or have the same professions. These 'subjects' become different objects to two minds that have grown old and have grown apart in considering them.[41]

Sylvia Sprigge, in her biography, records another instance of Berenson's recoil from Santayana, when the latter's death was reported: "There was something philistine about him, above all his Catholicism . . . something without pity and without humanity. He was utterly intellectual."[42] Philistinism we can set aside, I think. What Berenson surely meant, and resented, was that the experience of works of art was not the supreme value of existence for Santayana; and in this Santayana was at one with the Catholic Church. If one is to call his outlook "aesthetic," it will have to be in a sublimated and comprehensive sense of the word. "Without pity and without humanity" is unjust, I am convinced, but it touches an exposed flank.

Edmund Wilson visited Santayana just after the Second World War, when he had abandoned his plutocratic hotels, partly from force of circumstances and partly from a genuine preference for retrenchment and simplicity, and was living in a bed-sitter in the Nursing Home of the Blue Nuns on the Monte Celio in Rome. Wilson commented at one point in the article he subsequently wrote on Santayana that "I had mentioned in our conversation having recently met two persons of whom he had once seen a great deal, and had been struck by his total failure to show even a conventional interest in how they were or what they were doing."[43] Wilson perhaps makes too much of that. Is he not describing what is quite a common trait in old people? Santayana was over eighty. Wilson's quoting of a remark by Logan Pearsall Smith is rather more unsettling: "Santayana gives himself to you, pours out the rich stores of his mind, and forgets all about you the moment you leave the room. He doesn't dislike you, and doesn't like you or anyone else."

W. H. Auden touched on this reputed coldness in Santayana in a long and rather spiteful review written for *The New Yorker* in

1953[44] about the final volume of Santayana's autobiography, entitled *My Host the World*. He picked on Santayana's avowed preference for avoiding close personal entanglements, and his way of viewing existing individuals as the temporary lodging-places of desirable qualities: the eternal essences. Auden had some undergraduate fun with this: "Ah me, that delicious divine essence I met in Shanghai in 1906. . . . This divine essence isn't fun any more. I guess I better beat it." Santayana's manner of treating even his own self as an accidental contingency elicited a more solemn reproof from Auden: "I cannot be a spectator to my own life." Santayana thought otherwise: "I regard my occupations and interests somewhat as an actor regards his various parts or a painter his subjects."[45] The ultimate dignity of existence lay in transcending relativities, one's own included, within some comprehensive, detached yet charitable purview of the spirit.

Auden was still in full existentialist cry in the early 1950s, and Santayana's Greek espousal of essence instead of existence was naturally repugnant to him. It is significant that the whole existentialist furore which sprang up after the Second World War was fundamentally incomprehensible to Santayana, even though he did his best to keep up with what was going on, and had read with appreciation in earlier years the writings of figures antecedent to Existentialism, such as Husserl and Heidegger. The stress on "the Absurd" and the contingent in certain latter-day existentialists could conceivably have found an echo in Santayana's irrationalist doctrine of matter; he certainly read Shestov in the 1930s with some enthusiasm. But Santayana's attitude toward Existentialism after the Second World War suggests that he found most of its outlook perverse. If you insist on taking your personal fortunes as the centre of the universe, and your contingent choices as of cosmic import, naturally you will be in a state of *Angst*. Why do so?

As to *Angst* my quarrel with it is temperamental and you must not take it seriously. The reality is what Schopenhauer calls the Will, the Will to Live. It makes the child anxious to get the breast or the bottle, the lover his girl, the workman his Saturday night wages, and the invalid to get well. You can't help caring. But these natural cravings and fears are occasional, they can be modified or placated, you may "care" about something else. Latin poetry, for instance, which carries no *Angst* with it, though it is rich in interest and in *reassuring* knowledge of life. What I dislike about calling Will *Angst* is the suggestion that it is mysterious and non-natural. It is fundamental but can be appeased. It need not end in collapse but may be transcended throughout by charity and reason.[46]

Transcendence of *Angst*-ridden contingency always seemed possible to Santayana, even within the context of his own materialism. Such an act of transcendence is the mind's purest energy, "energia" in the Aristotelian sense, and its most fulfilling commitment. "For some temperaments," Santayana would doubtless have added. His relativism prevented him from legislating for the human race, and a guiding principle of all his thought was that each mode of being should find fulfilment in its own terms.

Fulfilment and serenity are the impressions most strongly conveyed by Edmund Wilson's account of his visit to Santayana. He tells us that he had "gotten the impression that Santayana was rather inaccessible," but found that the opposite was true. Wilson, with typical shrewdness, remarks at first that "I think he fancied himself in his role of monastic sage, and that his drab Franciscan dressing-gown was not perhaps altogether an accident." As he proceeds, Wilson's tone changes. Since his essay is the best personal account known to me of Santayana in old age, and since its predominantly admiring tone is notable, coming as it does from a man not easily impressed or fooled, I think it worth quoting at some length:

One of the wonderful things about him was the readiness and grace with which he played a classical role: that of the sage who has made it his business to meet and to reflect on all kinds of men and who will talk about the purpose and practice of life with anyone who likes to discuss them—as with me, whom he didn't know from Adam—since these are matters which concern us all. On his dignity and his distinction he did not need to insist: he let them take care of themselves; and his attitude toward a visitor—an attitude rather rare with the literary and the learned—was simply that of a man in the world who was trying to make some sense of it as you were. . . .

. . . One is, if anything, even more impressed by him after meeting him than one had been in reading those books. The image of him came back to me afterwards in the course of the solitary evenings that I spent when I was first in Rome: alone, with his plain table and his narrow bed, so far from Spain and from Harvard, yet with all the philosophies, the religions and the poetry through which he had passed making about him an iridescent integument, the manners of all the societies in which he had sojourned awhile supplying him with pictures and phrases; a shell of faded skin and frail bone, in which the power of intellect, the colors of imagination, still burned and gave out, through his books and his gentle-voiced conversation, their steady pulsations and rays, of which the intensity seems even to increase as the generator is more worn by use. I do not imagine he is troubled by the thought of death or that it even impinges as a shadow: his present so triumphant functioning appears to absorb and enchant him. . . .

. . . It would not be precisely true to say that Santayana is narcissistic, but he is interested in his own thought as a personal self-contained system, and in his life as a work of art which owes its integrity and harmony partly to a rigorous avoidance of indiscriminate human relationships.[47]

The impression of Santayana's personality as a perfectly fulfilled organism inhabiting the circle of its own achieved form, so well rendered by Edmund Wilson in those passages, is akin to what Wallace Stevens tried to convey about him in a brief comment in his essay "Imagination as Value," and in the elegy he wrote on the death of Santayana, entitled "To An Old Philosopher in Rome." Stevens knew Santayana slightly at Harvard; but his reactions are based on his writings, all of which Stevens reputedly possessed, and doubtless on hearsay concerning the blend of thought and life Santayana had achieved by his chosen mode of existence.

In the essay, written before Santayana died, having first made the point that "the existence of aesthetic value in lives that are forced on those that live them is an improbable sort of thing," Stevens goes on to say that

there can be lives, nevertheless, which exist by the deliberate choice of those that live them . . . it may be assumed that the life of Professor Santayana is a life in which the function of the imagination has had a function similar to its function in any deliberate work of art or letters. . . .

. . . We have only to think of this present phase of it, in which, in his old age, he dwells in the head of the world, in the company of devoted women, in their convent, and in the company of familiar saints, whose presence does so much to make any convent an appropriate refuge for a generous and human philosopher.[48]

"A generous and human philosopher"—the terms are to be noted, bearing in mind their distinguished and perceptive source, and bearing in mind, too, how easy it has often proved to brand Santayana as inhumanly selfish in outlook. Strident humanitarian sentiment is apt to be confused with depth of feeling. Santayana sought in persons and in civilisations the latent perfections to which the potentialities of their individual natures aspired, what Stevens called in his elegy "the celestial possible." With the empathy of a poet Stevens conveyed something of the struggle and the suffering entailed by the perfecting of any life. An aged philosopher in a Roman hospital room becomes an emblem of emergent form amid the confusions of existence:

> In a confusion on bed and books, a portent
> On the chair, a moving transparence on the nuns,
> A light on the candle tearing against the wick
> To join a hovering excellence, to escape
> From fire and be part only of that of which
>
> Fire is the symbol: the celestial possible.

Notwithstanding the urgent fragility conveyed by the image of light "tearing against the wick," Stevens writes at the poem's climax of Santayana as "the one invulnerable man among / Crude captains": the dominance of a comprehensive intellect and a sympathetic imagination achieving

> . . . a kind of total grandeur at the end
> With every visible thing enlarged and yet
> No more than a bed, a chair and moving nuns,
> The immensest theatre, the pillared porch,
> The book and candle in your ambered room,
>
> Total grandeur of a total edifice,
> Chosen by an inquisitor of structures
> For himself. He stops upon this threshold,
> As if the design of all his words takes form
> And frame from thinking and is realised.[49]

It was a favourite thought of Santayana that death, "by terminating a life, makes a biographical and moral finality of it."[50] Especially is this so when the energies latent in an organism have perfectly fulfilled themselves, so that there supervenes upon all the random accoutrements of dissolution a moral and spiritual finality. Cory's account of his last meeting with Santayana, who experienced great physical suffering at the end, has something of the quality of a scene depicted on a Greek stela, where disciple and master confront each other with resigned gravity. In this case the disciple broke down at one point. The master did not cease to pursue the round of his thoughts:

Our conversation turned, at his instigation, to the subject of death.

"What comes before or after does not matter," he said, "and this is especially so when one is dying. It is so easy for me now to see things under the form of eternity—and in particular that little fragment called my life."

By this time I was on the point of tears, but he went on to try and define more exactly the nature of death. I recall attempting some words of possible consolation.

"How about 'the peace that passeth all understanding'?" I mumbled.

After a moment or two he again shook his head in the manner that I knew so well. . . .

"If it passeth all understanding, it's simply nothing. I have no faith, nor find any comfort, in trying to imagine a blind cosmic feeling of peace."

There was a long pause, and he lay quiet with his eyes closed as if ready for sleep.

"Let's not discuss it any more, Cory," he finally said. "It's impossible to define in words. I prefer to be frankly poetical and say I am content to rest in the bosom of Abraham."

There was something so wonderful and calm about his voice that I broke down completely and sobbed like a child. I took his hand and pressed it hard against my lips, trying to control myself. Santayana was quite moved. I pulled myself together and apologised for being so sentimental.

"On the contrary," he replied, "it means a great deal to me. It shows that there must be a fundamental sympathy between us."

How he survived the last few days baffled the doctor and all the nurses. He had absolutely nothing to eat or drink. I only spoke to him once again, two days before the end. I had been sitting silently by his bed, when suddenly he started to move and groan as if in pain. Leaning forward over him, I asked him if he were suffering. I repeated the question several times before my voice penetrated the encircling gloom of consciousness. Then he replied in a voice so small that it seemed to come from a long distance:

"Yes, my friend. But my anguish is entirely physical; there are no moral difficulties whatsoever."

This calm final statement is imprinted like a die on the living tissues of my brain. Let his words speak for themselves, and they were uttered in the very jaws of a difficult death.[51]

There is an edge of asperity in Cory's last comments. He resented the apocryphal rumours of final anguished reconciliation between Santayana and the Catholic Church. That would have been insincere and inconsistent, two things Santayana never was. One may perhaps feel that Cory's imagination has in retrospect staged the final death-scene with too marmoreal a simplicity; equally, that the effect of a life being rounded off in perfectly appropriate terms was true to the total import of the situation, given the nature of the principal actor and Cory's habitual candour. The death of Socrates, more especially of Epicurus, could not have been far from the thoughts of either. It was a classical death, of intellectual dominion and perfected form, "the cancelling of the passions in the breast that includes them all, and their final subsidence beneath the glance that comprehends them."[52]

"What I have yearned for all my life," Santayana told Cory in the last year, "is not so much cosmic unity—like Whitehead, but simply 'completion.' If I see a circle half-drawn, I yearn to complete it."[53] Circularity was the traditional image for perfection, and Santayana's remark was significant. It showed how close he was to the spirit of antiquity, which strove always after the achieved outline in art, thought, and life. "The sphere of the soul is true to its own form," wrote Marcus Aurelius, "when it is neither extended in any way, nor contracted inwards, when it is neither scattered nor dies down, but is lighted by the light whereby it sees the truth of all things, and the truth within itself."[54] Words such as "scattered," "random," and "miscellaneous" occur frequently in Santayana's writings, and they always indicate the sorrowful distaste he felt at wasted energies, at matter striving vainly after its predestined form, at ideals incoherent and botched amid a tangle of undirected energies. Romanticism, liberalism, and industrial capitalism were thus passed in review in his early writings and condemned in the light of ideals he had derived from Plato and from Aristotle. Later in life, when passing judgement on his early *The Life of Reason,* he came to think that his drift had been too limited and moralistic. And indeed *The Life of Reason,* along with much of his other early writing, can be criticised for judging modern civilisation too exclusively in the light of an artificial and anachronistic Hellenism. The resemblance to Matthew Arnold was close.

In his later work there was a shift. Not in the direction of greater "relevance" to the age—how Santayana would have scorned that word if he had lived to experience its vogue!—but towards a more complete espousal of detached contemplation and a more tragic awareness of the inescapable plurality and distraction of existent being. He became more flexible in his later work simply because the mind of the sage must try to encompass being in its totality and not be governed by one transient ideal of perfection. "For spirit all times are equally present," he wrote, with an echo of Ranke, "and its proper and necessary lodging is, as the *Arabian Nights* have it, 'a city among the cities' and above all a heart among the hearts."[55]

Diversified sympathies did not, however, infringe upon the ultimate ideal of harmonious self-containedness. The urge to complete the circle never diminished, and the mature synthesis of Santayana's views, the four-volumed *Realms of Being,* prefaced by *Scepticism and Animal Faith,* with various outcroppings in the form of essays on political organisation, spiritual life, and New Testament themes, offers one of the most comprehensive systems of thought in the whole of twentieth-century philosophy. It is something of a paradox that this unfashionable predilection for synthesis and totality was displayed by a man devoid of belief that the processes of mind could comprehend the real nature of existence. In this Santayana was the antipodes of Hegel, who, along with his neo-idealist followers in America at the end of the nineteenth century, was always a special target of his criticism. Santayana was here in agreement with G. E. Moore and Bertrand Russell, who were doing a similar demolition job on British neo-Idealism. His links with them at the turn of the century, especially with Russell, were quite close.

Santayana's forte, however, was not the minute analysis of narrowly logical problems. There he diverged from Moore and Russell and from the predominant tendency of British and American philosophy in this century. He aimed rather at the rhetorical synthesis of a total vision of existence; but a system based, unlike Hegel's, on ultimately irrationalist premises. Those premises, he candidly admitted, were the expression of an organic disposition. His system of philosophy reflected the disposition, and his chosen way of life embodied the philosophy. Thus was the circle closed. The direction of the whole enterprise is aptly symbolised by the fact that his first prose work was a book on aesthetics, *The Sense of Beauty*. Perfected form took priority over analytical prowess. For that reason, philosophers of an analytic type will never take Santayana's work with entire seriousness. This was the case with Russell, who nevertheless clearly respected him. If anything, I shall exacerbate such a guarded response by the tenor of what follows, since I emphasise the imaginative basis of Santayana's vision of existence and look toward the wholeness of the effect rather than the minute integrity of the parts. A major fascination of his work lies in seeing how an irrationalist intuition into the nature of existence evolved over time into a comprehensive harmony internal to the solitary spirit. This arch-opponent of Hegel was perhaps more Hegelian than he realised.

·2·

Irrationalism and the Life of Reason: Earlier Writings

BERGSON in an essay called *Philosophical Intuition* remarked that any philosopher worthy of the name says only one thing; he says it because he knows only that one thing; and he mediates it in part through the imagery it generates or implies.[1] Bergson was referring primarily to philosophers who offer a systematic view of existence, with an inner coherence that makes the system self-sustaining and with all parts ultimately relevant to the single generative intuition. His main examples were Spinoza and Berkeley. Santayana's *Realms of Being* suggests such a system, even though on occasion he expressed a preference for calling it merely a "language." It has the air of impermeable self-sufficiency that one expects, fortified by a prose style that has calmly sustained eloquence even in fairly dry sections of analysis and rises naturally at climactic moments of insight to a heightened vein of imagery.

There is, however, a paradox intrinsic to these qualities in Santayana's mature philosophical system, *Realms of Being,* and it affects even our response to his earlier magnum opus, *The Life of Reason,* with its seemingly greater degree of rationalism. In the great rationalist or idealist ontologies the interlocking of the parts is a token that the mind is interpreting and reflecting a coherence, be it of one kind or another, that is intrinsic to the nature of being. The smooth internal coherence of the arguments transmitted onto the surface of Santayana's highly polished system, however, rested on a primary intuition that, even if mitigated, was fundamentally irrationalist. Acutely present to him always was the momentous contingency of existence, and

26

in many great passages of *Realms of Being* he conveyed with mythopoeic intensity the sovereign amplitude of that Realm of Matter which is the arena of all contingency. Santayana's philosophical vision was generated by an unnerving responsiveness to the threat of an ineluctable Something going its steady way beneath our busy human purposes and predications. "All things flow" beneath the frail bridges that human categories construct. In his early *The Life of Reason* Santayana called those categories "concretions in discourse." In his later philosophy the concretions in discourse became "essences," units of meaning that have an unstable connection with the obscure generative powers of matter, which they evoke or attempt to define; at best, a practical efficacy. The following passage is a central one for grasping Santayana's primary intuition into the ultimate nature of that Realm of Matter which is the sole sustaining cause of all that exists, and to which he applied the traditional metaphysical term of substance:

Substance, with its intrinsic deployment and heredity, would certainly remain mysterious to us even if we could inspect it at close quarters, because it involves an unintelligible alloy added to whatever essences we might assign to it. As things stand, however, the mystery is darkened by the great difference in scale between the texture of matter and that of human ideas; and when in mathematics, we pursue and almost seem to attain that inhuman reality, we find ourselves in possession of a perfect method of notation from which everything to be noted has disappeared; and the only truth of our most accurate science turns out to be practical and utterly blind. We must revert, in order to recover our sanity and the subject matter of our natural science, to crude experience and to the common arts; and here everything is on the human scale. Sunset and sunrise, the obvious repetitions in the generations of men and animals, and in their stock passions, hide movements which in nature are probably knit unbrokenly together, and never quite alike, or obedient to any disembodied law. Seen on the human scale, repetitions are perfectly inexplicable: they suggest to the gaping mind a magical control of events by a monotonous destiny: they suggest superstition. But beneath these trite measures, which human wit casts over things, like a net of proverbs, the natural flux goes its own pace, uncontrolled by any magic or logic. It is *natural:* it passes everywhere from what it was at that point, as the conjunction of elements there prompts it to do, never asking whether that conjunction is new or habitual. It knows no desire for novelty, no obsession by rule; it is as willing to run into repetitions as into catastrophes, and it is as likely to suggest to gross observation a law in one place as a purpose in another. Its order in one place may produce a mind to which its general order seems a chaos.[2]

It is worth remarking that near the beginning of the passage Santayana refers to mathematics as a perfect system of notation that is (almost) the ideal mode for attaining knowledge of the inhuman reality of substance. It suggests how close he was, in one respect, to the Cartesian tradition that viewed mathematics as an ideal of adequate knowledge. It reminds us, too, that before setting out to unfold his system of philosophy in the later *Realms of Being* Santayana prefaced it with an elaborate exercise in epistemological self-mutilation called *Scepticism and Animal Faith*. In it he ultimately reached what he called "a solipsism of the present moment" as being the only type of knowledge with a claim to the immediacy and certainty of intuition, which the Cartesian spirit has always pursued as an ideal of true knowledge. All claims to knowledge lacking such immediate and intuitive certainty are mere belief or, as Santayana preferred to call it, "animal faith." Yet, as the lengthy quotation from *The Realm of Matter* showed, Santayana never budged in his allegiance to the stubborn, persistent but obscure reality of a world outside the solipsistic consciousness. Concerning that world our knowledge is far from certain and intuitive; it is varied, indirect, and approximate. Hence all knowledge other than pure intuition is symbolic, not literal; but each mode of knowledge may be legitimate and efficacious in its own sphere and for its own purpose:

What is more evident than that religion, language, all the passions, and science itself speak in symbols; symbols which unify the diffuse processes of nature in adventitious human terms that have an entirely different aspect from the facts they stand for? In all these matters our thought works in a conventional medium, as the arts do.[3]

Santayana's writings abound in eloquent evocations of the "diffuse processes" of matter, and in them he sounds like a man confident of his own grasp of the deep truth of things. Strictly, there was no final cogency to his imperious evocations. Symbolic meanings, or essences, convey merely conventional human import, not truth. Doubtless aware of the difficult paradox, Santayana was prepared at times in *Realms of Being* to sit very lightly to any traditional notion of truth:

"And all that you yourself have written, here and elsewhere, about essence, is it not true?" No, I reply, it is not true, nor meant to be true. It is a grammatical or possibly a poetical construction having, like mathematics or theology, a certain internal vitality and interest; but in the direction of truth-finding, such constructions are merely instrumental like any language or any telescope. . . .

. . . There was a partial rationality or promise of rationality in things that encouraged the mind to clarify its ideas, and to develop logic. Logic is a child of fact, as spirit in general is a child of the psyche: a headstrong child quick to forget or deny the sweet milk that has nurtured it; yet the bond with earth remains notwithstanding. It remains not only in the past, fundamentally determining the choice of essences that logic shall play with, but it remains also contemporaneously, in that even the logician's thoughts are controlled at every turn by physical accidents and social pressure. . . .

. . . My thesis will therefore be a true thesis only in so far as in the realm of existence facts may justify my definitions and may hang together in the way that those definitions require. The case is the same in principle as in the homely equation, $2 + 2 = 4$; only that in arithmetic the terms are simpler and more familiar, so that the necessary relation between them is obvious to more people. It happens at the same time that the application of arithmetic, where it applies, is most constant and exact, so that its truth in those regions is beyond doubt; whereas any general logic applied to describing the universe, however ancient and well tried this logic may be, remains rather a form of human grammar. We are in a region of free intuition and construction, as in music, with no claims to propounding a revealed or a revealing truth.[4]

It is evident how easily such views can be accommodated to the sophisticated neo-Pragmatism advanced in recent years by Richard Rorty. Rorty in the concluding chapter of *Philosophy and the Mirror of Nature* places Santayana in the rather surprising company of "Goethe, Kierkegaard, William James, Dewey, the later Wittgenstein, the later Heidegger":[5] thinkers whom he dubs "edifying" and distinguishes from the many systematic philosophers in the Western tradition whom he considers unduly obsessed with a variety of single criteria of truth, or "privileged representations." In the upshot, Rorty sees philosophy no longer as an investigation into the true nature of reality, let alone as a spiritual discipline leading to the attainment of wisdom, but as a "conversation" in which philosophers become simply "people who are good at being human," not people who have "won through to truth." They will be "all-purpose intellectuals who are ready to offer a view on pretty much anything, in the hope of making it hang together with everything else."[6]

Even though Rorty's last sentence sounds like a downbeat statement close to the traditional undertaking of philosophy, the outlook has no real kinship to that of Santayana. Whatever the difficulties into which an initially sceptical theory of knowledge led him, Santayana was very much a traditional philosopher in setting himself up as a guide to the good life; and though he believed that human knowledge merely comprised a variety of efficacious symbols, he retained, possibly from his early theological formation, a firm reverence for the absolute nature of truth as the totality of realised essences.[7] He was really rather far from the off-handed deflations of a Rorty, in spite of resemblance in the area of epistemology. Perhaps a way of pinpointing the difference would be to say that Santayana was both pious and fervid fundamentally. The power and mystery evoked in his doctrine of Matter, and the aspirations espoused in his doctrine of Spirit, meant that he did not share the plain-suited preference for being an "all-purpose intellectual"; they put him in the company of those who see existence not as a series of analytical problems to be solved—or shelved—piecemeal, but as a predicament to be cloaked with an exalted wisdom. Santayana had the temperamental inclination toward comprehensiveness that is usually found in the great system builders of philosophy who believe in the primacy of mind or spirit in the total scheme of things, but in his case it was yoked to the irrationalist and sceptical presuppositions that have just been seen.

The most imposing instance of a great system-building philosophy in early modern times for which mind had primacy in the scheme of things was of course that of Hegel, with whom Santayana's relationship can be considered ambiguous. His overt hostility is well-known. He aligned Hegelian Absolute Idealism along with Romanticism as twin symptoms of the egotism, impiety, and anthropocentric conceit of modern Western civilisation. Yet despite Santayana's materialist hostility to Hegel's assertion of the primacy of mind, his own philosophical system culminated in a spiritual transcendence of the contingencies of time and history that bears a curious resemblance to Hegel's doctrine of Absolute Spirit, though admittedly Santayana wholly lacked that dynamic element of the dialectic which tempted Hegel to comprehend the whole dramatic structure of historical time within his own philosophical synthesis. Setting aside for the moment this paradoxical factor in their relationship, let us now by means of a group of quotations exemplify in as stark a manner as possible the primary intuition that governed the philosophy of Hegel, as distinct from that of Santayana. In the following sentences of Hegel we see how nature, which is other than thought, is nevertheless ultimately one of the stages of thought; thought in turn being invested with the attributes of God as it ceaselessly strives to effect the total rationalising of the real:

> The thinking view of nature must note the implicit process by which nature sublates its otherness to become spirit, and the way in which the Idea is present in each stage of nature itself. Estranged from the Idea, nature is merely the corpse of the understanding. Nature is the Idea, but only implicitly. That was why Schelling called it a petrified intelligence, which others have even said is frozen. God does not remain petrified and moribund however, the stones cry out and lift themselves up to spirit. God is subjectivity, activity, infinite actuosity, within which the other is only momentary, and remains implicit within the unity of the Idea, because it is itself this totality of the Idea. Since nature is the Idea in the form of otherness, according to the Notion of the Idea, the Idea is not within it as it is in and for itself, although nature is nevertheless one of the modes in which the Idea manifests itself, and in which it must come forth. . . .
>
> . . . In time nature comes first, but the absolute Prius is the Idea.[8]

> The problem of science, and especially of philosophy, undoubtedly consists in eliciting the necessity concealed under the semblance of contingency.[9]

Hegel there gives utterance in terms of his own system to what has been a widely held ambition of Western philosophy.

From the time when Parmenides, early in the fifth century before Christ, wrote that "it is the same thing to think and to be," European philosophy has been intermittently in thrall to a dream of reason. Metaphysicians as well as positivists have aimed by means of restricted and purified terminologies at grasping in a mental synthesis the totality of what shall count as true, or "really real." This ambition, so well clarified by Richard Rorty in recent years, has ranged from Spinoza's single substance inclusive of all determinations to a modest phalanx of atomistic data bolstered by an appropriate logic as found in some of the writings of Bertrand Russell and in the early Wittgenstein. Lev Shestov, a Russian religious existentialist of the early twentieth century who saw the nature of such an attitude very clearly, defined it in the following passage from his *Athens and Jerusalem* as the quest for some satisfying necessity in things that would reconcile them to the exigencies of reason:

> Since Socrates the truth, for men, has been confounded with universal and necessary judgments. Everyone is convinced that thought has the right to stop only when it has come up against Necessity, which puts an end to all searchings and all curiosity. And at the same time no one doubts that thought, in penetrating to the necessary relationships of things, accomplishes the supreme task of philosophy. So that Hegel, in short, saw quite rightly when he sought to demonstrate that there are not "philosophies" but "philosophy", that all the philosophers have always understood in the same way the mission that fate had imposed upon them. All of them sought to discover the rigorous and unchangeable order of being, for all of them—even those who, like Socrates, knew that they knew nothing—were completely hypnotized by the idea that this order which depends on no one must exist, that it is impossible that it should not exist, just as there must exist a science which reveals this order to man.[10]

Santayana always denied that there could be a science, a body of unified rational knowledge that shows the real order of being to the mind. And in this sense he was on the side of a whole irrationalist trend of modern thought exemplified by Shestov. At the same time, he was closer in a certain aspect of the early *Life of Reason* to the mood of Hegel than might have been expected, in spite of the fact that his primary intuition concerning the irrational contingency of existence and the determinative power of matter was the polar opposite of Hegel's. Upon such presuppositions, which fundamentally did not change throughout his career, Santayana nevertheless felt capable in his early years of erecting a superstructure of rationalistic humanism that was very attractive to many minds at the turn of the twentieth century who saw no cause to abandon reason to the physical scientists or the pure logicians.

The rest of the present chapter will give an impression of that earlier humanism of Santayana's *The Life of Reason,* with its debt not only to Hegel but also to Plato and to Aristotle. Before doing so it is worth noting the terms of his own assessment of the relation between his earlier and later outlook.

In a 1925 essay on John Dewey Santayana reproached him with exaggerating in his philosophy the "dominance of the foreground": an over-zealous concern, characteristically American, with the transforming power of human reason put to the service of practical energy. He contrasted this with "the old Ionians, or the Stoics or Spinoza or . . . those many mystics, Indian, Jewish, or Mohammedan who, heartily despising the foreground, have fallen in love with the greatness of nature and have sunk speechless before the infinite."[11] Just so the later Santayana may be said to have fallen in love with the greatness of Matter, and sunk, but not speechless, before the infinity of its substance. Santayana also discerned in Dewey's "dominance of the foreground" a link with the outlook of Hegel. For both, nature existed in order to serve consciousness, since "nature's parts are not (what they are in practice and for living animal faith) substances presenting accidental appearances. They are appearances integrally woven into a panorama entirely relative to human discourse." Such naturalism, Santayana added, "could not be more romantic"—seldom a favourable epithet with him. "Nature here is not a world but a story."[12] A panorama relative to human discourse is surely what nature did become for Hegel in his *Philosophy of Mind,* when he speaks of how "the Idea, or mind implicit, slumbering in Nature, overcomes externality, separateness, and immediacy, and creates for itself an existence conformable to its inwardness and universality, and thereby becomes mind which is inflected into itself and is for-itself, self-conscious or awakened mind, or mind as such."[13] If, however, we lay that sentence of Hegel alongside an opening section of *The Life of Reason,* we see that Santayana himself was not entirely remote from a Hegelian perspective in his early work, before a starker materialism had taken possession of him:

> The seed-bed of reason lies, then, in the immediate, but what reason draws thence is momentum and power to rise above its source. It is the perturbed immediate itself that finds or at least seeks its peace in reason, through which it comes in sight of some sort of ideal permanence. When the flux manages to form an eddy and to maintain by breathing and nutrition what we call a life, it affords some slight foothold and object for thought and becomes in a measure like the ark in the desert, a moving habitation for the eternal.[14]

The first two sentences of that passage are curiously Hegelian in the suggestion they carry that mind is the dramatic fulfilment and *raison d'être* of nature. They remind us that *The Life of Reason* was avowedly inspired by Hegel's *Phenomenology of Spirit,* its sub-title being "The Phases of Human Progress"; and although *The Life of Reason* is a series of timeless tableaux depicting the achievements of the mind in Art, Society, Religion, and Science, and not a dialectical drama of human spiritual progress throughout the course of history, Santayana may well seem to us in this phase of his career to stand in the company of those thinkers, like Hegel, who divinise humanity by making immanent in human reason the powers and prerogatives of God. "The Life of Reason, being the sphere of all human art, is man's imitation of divinity," as Santayana put it in the Introduction to his book on the topic.

There is not merely a smack of anthropocentric humanism along idealist lines in *The Life of Reason.* In it and in other early writings turns of phrase suggest the presence of an eager-eyed liberal-progressive of the 1900s; as when Santayana moots the possibility of an "Instauratio Magna" of human civilisation on more rational lines;[15] or when he writes that "the morrow may bring some great revolution in science," and "ventures to hope that religion and art may assume in the future forms far nobler and more rational than any they have hitherto worn";[16] or, at the end of *Three Philosophical Poets,* when he envisages the establishing of "a new religion and a new art, based on moral liberty and on moral courage."[17]

Given his later disposition, one can see why such things made him squirm. He remarked to Cory in the 1920s that he was

> very glad you don't like my earlier books. I read several passages in the *Life of Reason* last night about "Spirituality" and except for a phrase here and there, I thought them so bad that I am surprised people are so patient, and don't hoot at me in the street. It's only because they haven't read these slapdash random effusions, or not knowing anything about the subjects, can't feel how impertinent they are.[18]

And much later, when revising *The Life of Reason* in the last year of his life so as to remove what he himself called the early mists of Idealism that obscured its naturalism, he remarked:

> How optimistic in tone these volumes now seem to me! And how glib and cheeky in places! When I was a student and then a teacher at Harvard around the turn of the century, my friends and I really thought we had settled everything. We were sure, under the influence of Darwin, that science had come at last to replace religion. Of course we were wrong. Science is only a side development. It is far from being the whole story.[19]

The Life of Reason was the prime product of Santayana's earlier years, when so many talented young Americans revered him for offering a classical humanism fit for consumption in the modern world of post-Enlightenment progress. His later work was a sad disillusionment to many of them. The most telling recantation of his humanist ways in *The Life of Reason* is to be found in the Preface to *Dominations and Powers*, his late treatise on politics and society. The contrasting titles of the two works are illuminating: the one an expression of faith in harmonious control, the other of conviction that we are playthings of forces unamenable to human art or wit. The Santayana of *Dominations and Powers*, a work suffused with harsh biological wisdom concerning the varied species of human political animal, and eventually directing man away from the jungle toward the stars, passed judgement thus upon his earlier self:

> Many years ago, in the second volume of *The Life of Reason,* I drew a sketch of human society inspired by the ethics of Plato and Aristotle. I

was then a judicial moralist, distinguishing the rational use of institutions and deciding which were the best. If now I submit to the public some subsequent thoughts on the same subject, I do so with a more modest intention. I have become aware that anyone's sense of what is good and beautiful must have a somewhat narrow foundation, namely, his circumstances and his particular brand of human nature; and he should not expect the good or the beautiful after his own heart to be greatly prevalent or long maintained in the world. [20]

In the light of those remarks it seems clear that for an advantageous perspective on *The Life of Reason* and other early writings we must turn primarily not to Hegel but to the classical period of Greek philosophy.

Socrates by his probing dialectic stabilised the terms of moral evaluation, and Plato elevated those terms to a celestial status where they acted as beacons to guide mankind's wandering progress toward the harmonious fulfilment of its rational nature. Aristotle then rooted the moral goods of reason more firmly in the subsoil of human nature, but he, too, pruned and guided their growth toward their proper ends and purposes. Since both philosophers considered contemplation to be the true fulfilment of the rational nature of man, both were to affirm the supremacy of the intellectual element and to see the whole cosmos as a harmony of purposes culminating in a single principle superior to sense: the Form of the Good in Plato, and Aristotle's Unmoved Mover, the invisible magnet of all will and desire. In such a cosmic setting only did the classical strain of Greek philosophy find it possible to envisage a harmonious integration of human nature by the prudent nurturing of human instinct.

Santayana subscribed to the need for a single coherent will to integrate fluctuating human desires in some stable harmony, which is characteristic of classical eudaemonism and which persisted in the wider setting of medieval Catholicism, but he considered its elevation of teleological principles into the very structure of the cosmos to be mythical—"poetical physics"—and its detachment of the rational principle from matter as unacceptable to the empirical outlook of modern times. Accordingly he attempted to prune the extravagant outgrowths of

Greek rationalism that, by way of neo-Platonism, had merged with Christian supernaturalism, and to graft a classical and Catholic life of reason onto the harsher stock of modern materialism. Santayana's was never a mechanistic materialism on dogmatic nineteenth-century lines, however, but a poetic sense for the dynamic and fertile irrationality of the ultimate substance of things, such as Lucretius, a firm favourite of Santayana, had derived from the atomism of Epicurus.

In the opening sections of *The Life of Reason* Santayana recurrently stressed his primary intuition into the irrational basis of existence: "The chance fertility of nebulous objects, floating and breeding in the primeval Chaos."[21] Among these "tendencies afoot in nature"[22] there take shape over millions of years the complex centres of organisation we call human lives, which establish by chance adaptations an advantageous relation to the environment, the stabilising of their position having been facilitated by the emergence of consciousness that is "simply some partial natural harmony raising its voice and bearing witness to its own existence; to perfect that harmony is to round out and intensify that life."[23] From that original primitive "harmony"—Santayana made the word do a lot of work—are derived by slow degrees all the correlating and adaptive powers of reflection that we mean by a life of reason. They have enabled mankind, through experiment, to attain in certain fortunate phases of human civilisation the kind of stability that leads to happiness, which is

hidden from a free and casual will; it belongs rather to one chastened by a long education and unfolded in an atmosphere of sacred and perfected institutions. It is discipline that renders men rational and capable of happiness, by suppressing without hatred what needs to be suppressed to attain a beautiful naturalness. Discipline discredits the random pleasures of illusion, hope and triumph, and substitutes those which are self-reproductive, perennial and serene, because they express an equilibrium maintained with reality.[24]

The faintly menacing, level-eyed gaze of the Platonic philosopher-king blends in that final sentence with the patient assessment of the modern naturalist. Both would suggest that there is a rational moral regimen uniformly desirable for all men, although a little later in the same section of *The Life of Reason* this is qualified by the consideration of "extant interests" and by development being "impossible save in the concrete." An element of stark relativism was at the foundation of Santayana's work from the very beginning, but it was not fully coherent in the earlier, Platonic-Aristotelian phase of his thought. Clearly, too, it would not cohere with certain other types of ethical thought. The good for Santayana does not entail obedience to some law of pure duty in a noumenal sphere other than the natural, as with Kant. Nor is it much use to postulate "good" as a non-naturalistic, indefinable quality of which we have simple intuition. For Santayana, the good is simply the fulfilment of a specific nature, in the human instance an intellectual nature; and "everything ideal has a natural basis." [25] We do not hear much about the agony of moral choice, or even about conflict of interests, in *The Life of Reason*. The work is an ideal construct in which human nature is depicted as flowering into the realisation of its innate potential under the implied guidance of a practical wisdom that will harmonise all valid interests. And what constitutes "valid" interests is very much the difficult nub of the matter in any humanistic vision of the moral life grounded, like Santayana's, in naturalistic relativism.

G. E. Moore, hostile to what he called the "naturalistic fallacy" in ethics, is reported to have said that *The Life of Reason* was so confused that it was not worth discussing. We have this from Santayana himself, who wryly mentioned it to Cory when preparing in 1951 the revised version of *The Life of Reason*. The comment seems unfair. The work is perfectly clear and coherent on its own terms, but its terms are broadly enacted rather than minutely argued. All kinds of logical grit get absorbed into the smooth integument of Santayana's style, which carries hypnotic conviction in its epigrammatic concision, imaginative pressure, and rounded finality of cadence. His mind was primarily a visionary, synthesising medium rather than an instrument of analysis. He was the *poet* of reason. As such he was still finely attuned to the harmonies and sanctities of traditional European civilisation, Catholic as well as classical, and he drew no joy from either the practical or the ideological effects of secular progress in the nineteenth century, to which his formal naturalistic doctrines would logically seem to attach him.

The spirit of nineteenth-century positivism appeared to Santayana devoid of any coherent principles for fostering a life of reason: neither in art and social life nor in religion, which Santayana, like Matthew Arnold, was eager to preserve in some suitably qualified form. The fundamental impulse of positivist secularism had been a rebellious one, and the freedom in which it eventuated, that of agnostic liberals, was an empty freedom. It was understandable to strive for greater material well-being, but the restless energies unleashed were unfocussed by any more comprehensive rational goal and multiplied the machinery of existence to the detriment of its spiritual quality. The distractions of a rampant commercial and industrial civilisation

complicated life prodigiously without ennobling the mind. It has put into rich men's hands facilities and luxuries which they trifle with without achieving any dignity or true magnificence in living, while the poor, if physically more comfortable than formerly, are not meantime notably wiser or merrier. Ideal distinction has been sacrificed in the best men, to add material comforts to the worst. Things, as Emerson said, are in the saddle, and ride mankind. The means crowd out the ends and civilisation reverts, when it least thinks it, to barbarism.[26]

Santayana's critique in its broad outlines is almost tediously familiar from the vaticinations of like-minded Victorian sages in the middle and late nineteenth century, but it was more radically aristocratic and disillusioned than most. The mood was suavely penetrating and comprehensive rather than compassionate, apocalyptic, or earnestly hopeful of better things. It encompassed political libertarianism, plutocratic hubris, and the romantic cult of experience in a compendious dismissal and symbolised the whole in Goethe's Faust. All were a denial of limits and substituted worship of energy for docility to reason:

This saying—that the life possible and good for man is the life of reason, not the life of nature—is a hard one to the romantic, unintellectual, insatiable Faust. He thinks, like many another philosopher of feeling, since his is a part of the sum of experience, the whole of experience should be akin to his. But in fact the opposite is far nearer

the truth. Man is constituted by his limitations, by his station contrasted with all other stations, and his purposes chosen from amongst
all other purposes. Any great scope he can attain must be due to his
powers of representation. His understanding may render him universal; his life never can.[27]

"His understanding may render him universal; his life never
can." Thus did Santayana summon the resources of classic
wisdom to pass judgement on the aberrant vitality of the modern. The purest instances of such wisdom were for him Plato
and Aristotle, especially the latter, on account of the sturdier
biological origins of the Aristotelian life of reason. Santayana
might at first glance appear yet another Hellenising late Victorian, but I would be chary of saying of him what F. M. Turner
has said of Arnold:

What he meant by seeing things as they really are was not modern
scientific naturalism but rather a world-view that rested on fidelity to
nature—the *best* nature—and as a delicate discrimination of what this
best nature is: He sought to grasp not the laws as regularities of
physical nature but rather the intelligible law of things.[28]

Santayana sincerely tried to do both. He wanted to accommo-
date scientific naturalism and to derive from it values that, while
rooted in nature, would flower with the ordered inevitability of
classical perfections. He stressed the immanence in all growth of
specific natures to be realised, even though these were not
ordained by a providential or cosmic reason governing the
universe at large. The universal ideal for human nature implied
by Greek thought-structures later came to seem anachronistic to
Santayana, in the light of modern relativism and his own
increasingly individualistic detachment; but when at his best in
The Life of Reason he upheld it with a cool strength that was both
classic and modern. This passage about the man of unreasoned
life, from Plato's *Republic,* directs us to a major source of Santayana's inspiration:

Yes, I said, he lives from day to day indulging the appetite of the
hour; and sometimes he is lapped in drink and strains of the flute; then
he takes a turn at gymnastics; sometimes idling and neglecting everything, then once more living the life of a philosopher; often he is busy
with politics, and starts to his feet and says and does whatever comes

into his head; and, if he is emulous of any one who is a warrior, off he is in that direction, or of men of business, once more in that. His life has neither law nor order; and this distracted existence he terms joy and bliss and freedom; and so he goes on.

Yes, he replied, he is all liberty and equality.[29]

That comes from Book VIII of *The Republic,* where Plato shows how the worst characteristics of individual character may be writ large in the democratic mode of government. Santayana, like Plato, was aware of the anarchic ferment endemic to human nature and looked toward wise rulers and sane customs for moulding it into a harmonious shape. In principle Plato's mistrust of the random desires of the self ignorant of its own best interests could, like Hegel's similar mistrust, lead as easily to a socialist as to a conservative regimen. Santayana, an admirer of Plato, if not of Hegel, but always a friend of any incipient order amid the flux, was occasionally prepared to cast an unflurried glance at the political possibilities of socialism and communism in a world "saturated with the slow upward infiltration of a new spirit—that of an emancipated, atheistic, international democracy."[30] His spirit of dutiful detachment regarding communism and socialism was not really proof, however, against an innate preference for conservative societies and orthodox religious traditions. A mistrust of romantic deviants, heretics, revolutionaries, and liberals breathes through all his writings.[31] This was not based on some absolute norm in morals and politics. His ingrained individualism and relativism hardly permitted that, and they make him an ambiguous ally for twentieth-century neo-conservatism, where his name is sometimes called into service.[32] Certainly his conservative mistrust of the individual was no product of belief in the providential ordering of society or of some neo-Hegelian notion of the higher reason of the state. It was more akin to an aesthetic preference for order and harmony based on a conviction that religious and political traditions hallowed by long reckoning with the vagaries of human nature were best suited to foster in quietude the liberal arts and the contemplative virtues at which all good government should aim. Customary settled ways, and the language of evaluation that expressed them, are the firm, well-knit products of organic growth; their existence calls for no extraneous justification in terms of natural rights or social contracts. Santayana's Life of Reason was not a Life of Rationalism.

For Santayana, a social order was justified by its fruits, not by its origins. The fruits of an aristocratic society at its best have been fine manners, beautiful settings, liberal arts, and civilised subtleties of mind. They are the products of concentration and distillation. To diffuse them is to dilute them:

Ideal goods cannot be assimilated without some training and leisure. Like education and religion they are degraded by popularity, and reduced from what the master intended to what the people are able and willing to receive. So pleasing an idea, then, as this of diffused ideal possessions has little application in a society aristocratically framed; for the greater eminence the few attain the less able are the many to follow them. Great thoughts require a great mind and pure beauties a profound sensibility. To attempt to give such things a wide currency is to be willing to denaturalise them in order to boast that they have been propagated. Culture is on the horns of this dilemma: if profound and noble it must remain rare, if common it must become mean. These alternatives can never be eluded until some purified and high-bred race succeeds the promiscuous bipeds that now blacken the planet.[33]

The desirable fruit of Reason in Society is the high culture of an élite. Not the restless international plutocracy coming to prominence in capitalist societies of the West in the late nineteenth century, not much liked by Santayana, but something akin to the ideal of Yeats in "A Prayer for My Daughter":

How but in custom and in ceremony
Are innocence and beauty born?
Ceremony's a name for the rich horn,
And custom for the spreading laurel tree.

Yeats, however, could be silly and snobbish in his traditionalism. Santayana never was. The spiritual egalitarianism so deeply rooted in Spanish character saved him. He recounts approvingly in a volume of his autobiography an anecdote about Arthur Strong, an authority on Moorish civilisation:

He reminded me of my father. Through the Moors he had good knowledge of Spain also: and he said something about the Spanish mind that has given me food for reflection. "The Spaniard," he said, "respects only one thing, and that is—," and he raised his forefinger, pointing to heaven. There is no power but Allah: he is omnificent, and all appearances and all wills are nought. It is quite true that no genuine or reflective person in Spain trusts anybody or is proud of himself. He may be vain and punctilious, but that is play-acting: he thinks that pose is set down for him in his rôle; but inwardly he knows that he is dust. This is the insight that I express by saying to myself that the only authority in existence is the *authority of things*. I like the irony and blessedness of this: that since only *things* have any authority there is, *morally,* no authority at all, and the spirit is free in its affections.[34]

"The spirit is free in its affections." The impartiality of disillusion makes inherited traditions ultimately just as arbitrary as radical dogmas of progress. No snob, conservative or radical, sees things in this light. Santayana's liking for the grand forms of aristocratic society carried with it no inherent spiritual sanction. It was simply a congenital preference for harmony in strength; if that harmony in strength could be joined with something of ease and informality, as in the English version of aristocratic life, so much the better. Santayana's ideal was close to that of Plato. It was the ideal of the "kalokagathos," blending beauty and goodness in a character harmonised through the nurture of sound traditions.[35] Santayana tells in his autobiography of a visit to Winchester College in the company of Frank Russell, Bertrand Russell's brother, a close friend of his at the turn of the century. There can surely be few more touching and dignified evocations of the atmosphere in which a youthful "kalokagathos" is bred:

In the evening I went again to the chapel. This time I was alone, and from my corner I drank in the memorable spectacle, more memorable for being something usual and the crown of every school day. The boys were less restless at that hour; fatigue and darkness cut off distractions; the spirit of the place, the language of the prayers, had a chance of attuning the senses to their ancient music. That everything external was perfunctory rather helped something internal to become dominant. I saw some boys bury their faces in their folded arms, not (it seemed to me) affectedly, but as if seeking solitude, as if fleeing to the wilderness, carried by a wave of juvenile devotion. How well I knew that plight! Adolescence, in its pregnant vagueness, casts about for some ineffable happiness in the fourth dimension. But how admirable the setting here to give a true pitch to those first notes! This simplicity in wealth protects from vulgarity, these classic poets, when grammar and ferrule are forgotten, leave a sediment of taste and soundness in the mind, and these reticent prayers, with their diplomatic dignity and courtesy, leave it for the heart to say the last word. It is all make-believe, as sports are: but in both those dramatic exercises there is excellent discipline, and the art of life is half learned when they have been practised and outgrown. What has been learned is the right manner, the just sentiment; it remains to discover the real occasions and the real risks.[36]

Santayana particularly admired in traditional English life the protection given by codes and forms to the integrity of the inner self. That self could be pensive and shifting and fundamentally alone, but a settled tradition of easy formality maintained the right diplomatic links with the outer world and gave coherence to the random episodes of existence: "the right manner, the just sentiment." "Happiness," as Santayana had written elsewhere, "is hidden from a free and casual will; it belongs rather to one chastened by a long education and unfolded in an atmosphere of perfected institutions."[37]

From the vignette of that scene in Winchester chapel we also catch a revealing glimpse of Santayana's attitude to orthodox religious tradition. "It is all make-believe," taken literally, but as a help to steering a steady course amid the currents of existence, under the tutelage of hallowed ideals that are the fruits of ancient spiritual insight, it is an admirable discipline and an essential component of the Life of Reason. Such ideals confront one in traditional religion "with clearness and authority,"[38] and we gain from them that chastening sense of dependence on a power not ourselves, which is piety. Santayana's attitude to religion in his early writings is much like that of Matthew Arnold. It is seen as an expression of human ideals. Perhaps the most completely reasonable one if we accept Santayana's view of reason as an encompassing harmony. But no more than that.

"Religion," wrote Karl Barth in ringingly opposite terms,

is aware that it is in no wise the crown and fulfilment of true humanity; it knows itself rather to be a questionable, disturbing, dangerous thing. . . . Religion, so far from being the place where the healthy harmony of human life is lauded, is instead the place where it appears diseased, discordant and disrupted.[39]

Santayana was no stranger to the idea that life is "diseased, discordant and disrupted." An innate pessimistic bent, along with the doctrine of sin imbibed from a Catholic upbringing, had seen to that. In much of his autobiography written in old age, as well as in the mature synthesis of *Realms of Being* and *Dominations and Powers,* a sense of the extremity of the human predicament is constantly present. Despite his inflexible refusal to make any formal commitment to faith, Santayana's later work constitutes one of the most radical instances of a religious attitude to existence in twentieth-century Western culture—almost radical enough in spiritual elevation to confront on its own peculiar terms the searing utterance of Karl Barth. In *The Life of Reason* only one chapter revealed this potential in Santayana's nature. It is called "Post-Rational Morality." In it Santayana reviewed a variety of other-worldly "experiments in redemption" that signify despair of realising a rational earthly society; he found such mystically resigned doctrines consoling, but "somewhat cheap." In his later work he propounded one of his own. It rings truer than the late Victorian compromise of *Reason in Religion.*

In that work and in other early writings Santayana's position was more vulnerably bland. Religion viewed simply as an ideal propounded by the human spirit, and then subsumed in the overarching harmonies of a life of reason, is on the same footing as art and poetry; religion having a fatal propensity for taking its own myths too seriously, a fanaticism to be deplored. Like poetry, however, religion in its proper functioning correlates the impulses of human nature and focusses them in symbols that harmonize the will and illuminate the spirit. The outlook was distinctly Arnoldian. A work by Santayana that preceded the publication of *The Life of Reason* was entitled *Interpretations of Poetry and Religion.* The parity of the two suggested in the title is consistently exemplified throughout the essays, which continue to impress by their classical grasp of the moral disposition of an author and of the way in which that disposition can be betrayed by formal incoherence and fragmentation:

The spirit of life, innocent of any rationalising discipline, relapses into miscellaneous and shallow exuberance. Religion and art become short-winded. . . . The poetry of barbarism is not without its charm.

It can play with sense and passion the more readily and freely in that it does not aspire to subordinate them to a clear thought or a tenable attitude of the will.[40]

For Santayana, Browning and Whitman were salient examples of romantic turbulence and incoherence, in love with the incurably accidental vividness of experience rather than its ideal consummations. Aestheticism was the trivialised end product of Romanticism. In his famous essay on Whitman and Browning, "The Poetry of Barbarism," his grasp of their qualities, which for him are nearly all defects, is magnificently incisive and comprehensive—a model of criticism that distils the human essence of literature rather than estranges its urgency by solipsistic ingenuities of formal analysis. Yet Santayana's implied alternative to the poetry of barbarism could in practice be the kiss of death for any vital art, like Arnold's neo-classical ideal in the 1853 Preface to his own poems, to which Santayana's early essays on poetry bear a strong resemblance. Might one not say of him what Denis Donoghue said of Arnold, that he "wanted ideas to deliver him from the bewilderment and the insecurity of experience"?[41] Admittedly Santayana's ideal of art in its highest reaches sounds rather splendid, when abstractly stated in the wider context of *Reason in Art,* the fourth volume of *The Life of Reason,* and the attractiveness of the theory is by no means obviously that of elevated escapism, which Donoghue sensed in Arnold. In fact, it pointedly sets itself against romantic or aesthetic flights from reality:

To exalt fine art into a truly ideal activity we should have to knit it more closely with other rational functions, so that to beautify things might render them more useful and to represent them most imaginatively might be to see them in their truth. Something of the sort has been actually attained by the noblest arts in their noblest phases. A Sophocles or a Leonardo dominates his dreamful vehicle and works upon the real world by its means. These small centres, where interfunctional harmony is attained, ought to expand and cover the whole field. Art, like religion, needs to be absorbed in the Life of Reason. . . .
    . . . If the fine arts express moral and political greatness, and serve to enhance it, they acquire a certain dignity; but so soon as this expressive function is abandoned they grow meretricious. The artist becomes an

abstracted trifler, and the public is divided into two camps: the dilet-
tanti, who dote on the artist's affectations, and the rabble, who pay him
to grow coarse. Both influences degrade him and he helps to foster
both. An atmosphere of dependence and charlatanry gathers about the
artistic attitude and spreads with its influence. Religion, philosophy,
and manners may in turn be infected with this spirit, being reduced to a
voluntary hallucination or petty flattery. Romanticism, ritualism, aestheticism, symbolism are names this disease has borne at different
times as it appeared in different circles or touched a different object. . . . Art as mankind has hitherto practised it . . . too much
resembles an opiate or a stimulant.[42]

From that rather pursed lips reference to opiates and stimu-
lants we divine something of the appeal that Santayana's early
writings on literature at one time possessed for F. R. Leavis and
some of his associates. Q. D. Leavis wrote, "Literary criticism
for him is not in the least a game with poetry as counters but
supremely a matter of evaluating, of relating poetry to culture,
tradition and human experience."[43] William Walsh tells us that
"Santayana had no patience with aestheticism"—which is true
in a limited sense—and, rather more implausibly, that he had "a
profound acceptance and reverence for life."[44] Nearer the mark
was the anonymous reviewer of a selection from Santayana's
literary criticism who wrote that "Santayana represents a curious triumph of civilisation bought at the cost of a withdrawal
which in the end makes communication nearly impossible."[45]
That puts it too strongly, of course. But the writer correctly
sensed even in Santayana's early work a detachment from existence that always made him a dubious inspiration for cultural
critics propagating a selective and moralistic version of the
English tradition. No wonder the Leavisites eventually sheered
off. When in Santayana's later philosophy moralising rationalism receded, the note of Downing-College-by-the-Ilissus also
died away in his attitude to the arts. He came to value the free
play of intuition among beautiful essences for its own sake, as a
sign of the spirit's inner freedom.[46]

The irony of Santayana's earlier rejection of aestheticism and
of what one critic has called his virtual rejection of fine art as
such, for the sake of art's function within the larger utility of the
Life of Reason,[47] is that it took place in the context of a philo-

sophical system that even in its *Life of Reason* phase was at heart a
more comprehensive and aspiring type of aestheticism. Take this
paragraph from the penultimate chapter of *Reason in Art:*

> If the rendering of reality is to remain artistic, it must still study to
> satisfy the senses; but as this study would now accompany every
> activity, taste would grow vastly more subtle and exacting. Whatever
> any man said or did or made, he would be alive to its aesthetic quality,
> and beauty would be a pervasive ingredient in happiness. No work
> would be called, in a special sense, a work of art, for all works would
> be such intrinsically; and even instinctive mimicry and reproduction
> would themselves operate, not when mischief or idleness prompted,
> but when some human occasion and some general utility made the
> exercise of such skill entirely delightful. Thus there would need to be
> no division of mankind into mechanical blind workers and half-
> demented poets, and no separation of useful from fine art, such as
> people make who have understood neither the nature nor the ultimate
> reward of human action. All arts would be practised together and
> merged in the art of life, the only one wholly useful or fine among
> them.[48]

It is indeed odd to hear the sceptical, pessimistic Santayana
uttering words that recall the nobly fatuous utopianism of a
William Morris about future communities of free and beautiful
people. That is the "1900s" side of Santayana with a vengeance,
and an instance of the kind of thing he himself later came to
dislike so intensely in *The Life of Reason*. Viewed in another
light, the passage is revealing. It suggests that the harmonious
ideal forms of great art are a model for the good life as such.

> If happiness is the ultimate sanction of art, art in turn is the best
> instrument of happiness. In art more directly than in other activities
> man's self expression is cumulative and finds an immediate reward; for
> it alters the conditions of sentience so that sentience becomes at once
> more delightful and more significant.[49]

> Beauty therefore seems to be the clearest manifestation of perfection,
> and the best evidence of its possibility. If perfection is, as it should be,
> the ultimate justification of being, we may understand the ground of
> the moral dignity of beauty. Beauty is a pledge of the possible confor-
> mity of soul and nature, and consequently a ground of faith in the
> supremacy of the good.[50]

Conformity of soul and nature as the culminating achievement of reason is a nice gloss of Santayana's ideal of harmony, and *The Life of Reason* may well strike us as itself an emblem of the harmony it proposes: an elaborate and euphonious construct offering to our imagination an elevated group of ideal possibilities betokening the mind's transcendence of the chaotic flux of matter and ability to live most fully in the presence of "beautiful idealisms of moral excellence." Shelley's phrase seems the apt one. One can only agree with the critic who wrote, "Compared to this, the aestheticism of a Pater or a Berenson remains meagre and half-hearted." [51]

Santayana's aesthetic reconstruction of classical eudaemonism reposed on frail foundations. For is not the integrity of the moral life ultimately dependent upon a firmer rational basis in the nature of things than Santayana can provide? Alasdair MacIntyre, making a sortie beyond the logical sphere to which recent English-speaking moral philosophers have tended to confine themselves, has made this point in his book, *After Virtue*. He maintains that without a teleological framework in the classical, Aristotelian tradition—whether in its Greek or medieval versions—"the whole project of morality becomes unintelligible," [52] and that "moral judgements are linguistic survivals from the practices of classical theism which have lost the context provided by those practices." [53] By classical theism one would understand some such scheme of values as St. Thomas Aquinas took from classical eudaemonism and harmonised with the revealed faith of Christianity. Moreover, without the latter element Jacques Maritain was inclined to see even classical eudaemonism as a kind of corporate hedonism ignorant of the transcendent source of duty and love. [54]

Such views, acceptable or not, sharpen the angle of vision upon Santayana. He had no metaphysics in the traditional sense of seeing existence as grounded in rational principles. He candidly admitted that all values were focussed in the self and ultimately relative to that centre, though capable of "harmonising" with other centres of self and of issuing in a "Life of Reason." [55] Hence I think the ultimately factitious impression conveyed by that work, despite all its beauty, wisdom, and common sense: a *tour de force* of rational humanism by a relativistic materialist, who had not yet canalised the powerful current of his religious nature. His later writings, especially *Realms of Being, Platonism and the Spiritual Life,* and *Dominations and Powers,* fulfil the exigencies of that strange nature in a more convincing way. The polish and brilliance are still there in the later books; Santayana remains almost too quotable. But their eloquence is more authentically rapt. Something smug hovers over much of *The Life of Reason* and the other earlier books. Michael Oakeshott's phrase gets it very well: "precocious sagacity."

There is, however, a doctrinal aspect of *The Life of Reason* that authentically prefigures the later Santayana, and it is best caught by a couple of sentences from *Reason in Common Sense.* Santayana remarks that ideal terms, the units of rational meaning which he later called "essences," "remain always remote from natural existence, and the latter irreducible to a logical principle."[56] He says, "We undergo events, we grow into character, by the subterranean working of irrational forces that make their incalculable irruptions into life none the less wonderfully in the revelations of man's heart to himself than in the cataclysms of the world around him."[57] Here we touch again upon the primary intuition that governed the whole of Santayana's philosophical vision: the irrational, obscure principle of matter that is constantly in flux and that, though intermittently forming eddies of rational equilibrium, is itself the determining power of all the meanings we may chance to give it. Hegel, too, had this intuition of the contingent, to a greater extent than he is usually given credit for, as when he wrote,

It is not only that in nature the play of forms has unbounded and unbridled contingency, but that each shape by itself is devoid of its Notion. *Life* is the highest to which nature drives in its determinate being, but as merely natural Idea, life is submerged in the irrationality of externality, and the living individual is bound with another individuality in every moment of its existence.[58]

In the motley play of the world, if we may so call the sum of existents, there is nowhere a firm footing to be found: everything bears an aspect of relativity, conditioned by and conditioning something else . . . and therefore the craving of the reason after knowledge passes with the further development of the logical Idea beyond this position of mere relativity.[59]

The "craving of the reason" to which Hegel refers is something that his own system wholly satisfies: sheer externality can be incorporated into the workings of consciousness and thereby raised to its true concrete individuality. For Santayana, this is not so. Our rational dialectic may have its own dreamlike coherence, and we may aspire to dwell spiritually amid such of its elements as are congenial to our temperaments—as when we write books on "The Life of Reason." But those meanings are of another realm, logical and timeless. Santayana was later to call it the Realm of Essence. He made a sharp disjunction between matter, which is obscure, inchoate, and omnipotent, and essence, or form, which is clear, determinate, and impotent. This led him into the logical difficulty of accounting for the interaction of the two realms of essence and existence endemic to any type of Platonic dualism. The nerve of that later dualism, however, was moral and imaginative rather than logical, and it must be seen in the context of a philosophy that only fully unfolded its inner principle through time and under the stimulus of events in the outer world. *The Life of Reason* and other earlier writings we have been considering, which attempted to fuse Greek rationalism and modern materialism within the context of an early twentieth-century faith in progress, fall back into the wider and darker space of his later views. The First World War seems to have crystallised the predominantly irrationalist impulse of those later views, as well as accentuated Santayana's spiritual isolation and detachment. Release from a professorship at Harvard may also have helped him to find himself.

In one of his *Soliloquies in England* he describes how on Armistice Day he chanced to be in a coffee-house at Oxford. Some young wounded officers started to sing the old tune of "Tipperary," stirred by their release from war and the prospect of a better world. The passage is worth quoting at some length:

You suppose that this war has been a criminal blunder and an exceptional horror; you imagine that before long reason will prevail, and all these inferior people that govern the world will be swept aside, and your own party will reform everything and remain always in office. You are mistaken. This war has given you your first glimpse of the ancient, fundamental, normal state of the world, your first taste of reality. It should teach you to dismiss all your philosophies of progress or of a governing reason as the babble of dreamers who walk through one world mentally beholding another. I don't mean that you or they are fools; heaven forbid. You have too much mind. It is easy to behave very much like other people and yet be possessed inwardly by a narcotic dream. I am sure the flowers—and you resemble flowers yourselves, though a bit wilted—if they speculate at all, construct idealisms which, like your own, express their inner sensibility and their experience of the weather, without much resemblance to the world at large. Their thoughts, like yours, are all positings and deductions and asseverations of what ought to be, whilst the calm truth is marching on unheeded outside. No great harm ensues, because the flowers are rooted in their places and adjusted to the prevailing climate. It doesn't matter what they think. You, too, in your lodgings in Chelsea, quite as in Lhasa or in Mount Athos, may live and die happy in your painted cells. It is the primitive and ultimate office of the mind to supply such a sanctuary. But if you are ever driven again into the open, if the course of events should be so rapid, that you could catch the drift of it in your short life (since you despise tradition), then you must prepare for a ruder shock. There is eternal war in nature, a war in which every cause is ultimately lost and every nation destroyed. War is but resisted change; and change must needs be resisted so long as the organism it would destroy retains any vitality. Peace itself means discipline at home and invulnerability abroad—two forms of permanent virtual war; peace requires so vigorous an internal regimen that every germ of dissolution or infection shall be repelled before it reaches the public soul. This war has been a short one, and its ravages slight in comparison with what remains standing: a severe war is one in which the entire manhood of a nation is destroyed, its cities razed, and its women and children driven into slavery. In this instance the slaughter has been greater, perhaps, only because modern populations are so enormous; the disturbance has been acute only because the modern industrial system is so dangerously complex and unstable; and the expense seems prodigious because we were so extravagantly rich. Our society was a sleepy glutton who thought himself immortal and squealed inexpressibly, like a stuck pig, at the first prick of the sword. An ancient city would have thought this war, or one relatively as costly, only a normal incident; and certainly the Germans will not regard it otherwise.

Existence, being a perpetual generation, involves aspiration, and its aspiration envelops it in an atmosphere of light, the joy and the beauty of being, which is the living heaven; but for the same reason existence, in its texture, involves a perpetual and living hell—the conflict and mutual hatred of its parts, each endeavouring to devour its neighbour's substance in the vain effort to live for ever. Now, the greater part of most men's souls dwells in this hell, and ends there. One of their chief torments is the desire to live without dying—continual death being a part of the only possible and happy life. We wish to exist materially, and yet resent the plastic stress, the very force of material being, which is daily creating and destroying us.[60]

That is a cruelly elegiac passage. Yet—saving the gift of a providentially revealed religion—can one easily gainsay its painful element of truthfulness? Admittedly there is passing allusion to the fact that existence involves aspirations to joy and beauty, as well as suggestion that these may fleetingly be realised. The harmonies of the life of reason still have their pertinence, as *Dominations and Powers,* Santayana's late treatise on politics and society, will make clear. He may have been a "pessimist," for what such declamatory definitions are worth, but he was not a nihilist; or if so, only in some qualified fashion. Yet progressively harmonious social good was clearly not the principal good envisaged by a man who wrote that lengthy passage about the young soldiers and "Tipperary." Inspiration has passed from the outer to the inner sphere. Santayana has moved away from the humanism and the optimistic rationalism of post-Enlightenment Western civilisation, overtones of which are to be heard in *The Life of Reason* and his other early writings, toward a personal system of thought more integral to his peculiar temperament. Among its eclectic components are a materialism akin to some of the pre-Socratic philosophies of ancient Greece; a spirituality blending the self-sufficiency of a Hellenistic sage with Eastern ideals of gnosis and liberation; and an individualism rooted in the *contemptus mundi* outlook of Spanish Catholic tradition. All Spaniards, Unamuno remarked, feel that the individual is the end for which the universe exists.[61] "Yo para Dios y Dios para mi, y no más mundo"![62]

Unamuno gave his imaginary archetype of the Spaniard a mystical dimension in *The Tragic Sense of Life:* such a being feels so passionately his singular concrete existence in the flesh that he scorns rational systems of philosophy and craves above all else the resurrection of both body and soul by the aid of some desperate Kierkegaardian venture of faith—a venture he can never quite manage to bring off. One does nevertheless sense, as a factor shared with Santayana, Unamuno's pessimistic scorn of the world and the social good, and his compensating stress on individual salvation. Compatible with this cultural stereotype are the views of Angel Ganivet, to whom Unamuno refers in *The Tragic Sense of Life,* and who was another of the so-called Generation of '98 in Spanish cultural history. Ganivet's pessimistic scepticism entailed withdrawal into a stoical self-sufficiency deeply characteristic of the radical soul of Spain, and he even traced it back to Seneca, whose origins were "Spanish." There is some point in relating Santayana to a Spanish background rather than always placing him in the American context of New England and Harvard. He kept up his contacts with Spain during his American years through visits and correspondence with his father[63] and, more particularly, with his devoutly Catholic half-sister, Susana, after she had abandoned Boston and returned to the family's native Spain. Santayana also cultivated, rather self-consciously perhaps, the alien perspective of a Latin and a Spanish Catholic in relation to American concerns when at Harvard, and both then and thereafter never ceased to be concerned about the fortunes and misfortunes of a country whose citizenship he retained throughout his entire life.

In an early sonnet of Santayana the closing lines catch well both his isolation in America and his compassionate disdain for human striving. The marmoreal preciosity of their cadence is typical of much of his poetry. He never set great store by his verses, but claimed that they were always sincere. This we need not doubt:

> Sweet are the days we wander with no hope
> Along life's labyrinthine trodden way,
> With no impatience at the steep's delay,
> Nor sorrow at the swift-descended slope.
> Why this inane curiosity to grope
> In the dim dust for gems' unmeaning ray?
> Why this proud piety, that dares to pray
> For a world wider than the heaven's cope?
> Farewell, my burden! No more will I bear

> The foolish load of my fond faith's despair,
> But trip the idle race with careless feet.
> The crown of olive let another wear;
> It is my crown to mock the runner's heat
> With gentle wonder and with laughter sweet. [64]

Such epicurean detachment set Santayana apart from the mood of America and Harvard at the turn of the century. When, in spite of incidental praise, Santayana sensed that William James reacted unfavourably to the Latin disenchantment and Platonic Idealism of *The Life of Reason,* he reproached James in a letter with not having felt in it

> something which, I am sure, is there: I mean the *tears.* . . . It is not the past that seems to me affecting, entrancing or pitiful to lose. It is the ideal. It is that vision of perfection that we just catch, or for a moment embody in some work of art, or in some idealised reality. . . . And it is my adoration of this real and familiar good, this love often embraced but always elusive, that makes me detest the Absolutes and the dragooned myths by which people try to cancel the passing ideal, or to denaturalise it. [65]

"The *passing* ideal," Santayana writes. The phrase reminds us that Santayana had learned much from William James about the swift transience of the experiential flux and hinted at a qualification of his Platonic Idealism. Yet I doubt whether the qualification would have impressed James; and I do not think those tears would have been a recommendation to him. Santayana's theory of knowledge can easily be given a pragmatist turn, and his naturalism—he preferred to call it "materialism"—would seem to align him with James, Dewey, and the whole shift away from metaphysics in early twentieth-century American philosophy. Yet read a typical passage in which James moves from a technical point about pragmatist truth, with whose relativist drift Santayana might have been in rough agreement, to a wider vision of things. We see at once that agreement on technical issues is of small account, given a fundamental disparity of temperament:

> The humanism, for instance, which I see and try so hard to defend is the completest truth attained from my point of view up to date. But, owing to the fact that all experience is a process, no point of view can

ever be *the* last one. Every one is insufficient and off its balance and responsible to later points of view than itself. . . .

. . . From the fact that finite experiences must draw support from one another, philosophers pass to the notion that experience *überhaupt* must need an absolute support. The denial of such a notion by humanism lies probably at the root of most of the dislike which it incurs.

But is this not the globe, the elephant, and the tortoise over again? Must not something end by supporting itself? Humanism is willing to let finite experience be self-supporting. Somewhere being must immediately breast nonentity. Why may not the advancing front of experience, carrying its immanent satisfactions and dissatisfactions, cut against the black inane as the luminous orb of the moon cuts the caerulean abyss? Why should anywhere the world be absolutely fixed and finished? And if reality genuinely grows, why may it not grow in these very determinations which here and now are made?[66]

There is a robust exuberance to James's prose, very different from the smooth distillations of Santayana. The rhythms of the concluding section are open, visionary, aspiring. Santayana always managed to sound lapidary. James's antipathy to what is "fixed and finished" is a link with Dewey, and Santayana explained his own estrangement from Dewey by writing that

the master-burden of his philosophy, which lends it its national character, is a profound sympathy with the enterprise of life in all lay directions, in its technical and moral complexity, and especially in its American form, where individual initiative, although still demanded and prized, is quickly subjected to overwhelming democratic control.[67]

That in turn may remind us of a passage in which Santayana commented on the academic environment at Harvard in the early part of this century, in which

a slight smell of brimstone lingered in the air. You might think what you liked, but you must consecrate your belief or your unbelief to the common task of encouraging everybody and helping everything on. You might almost be an atheist, if you were troubled enough about it. The atmosphere was not that of intelligence nor of science, it was that of duty.[68]

Duty consisted in being continuously hopeful about the common enterprise of investigation in which one was engaged as part of the unfolding spirit of progressive humanity. Royce, the belated exponent of Hegelian Idealism, on whom Santayana wrote one of his more stringent essays in *Character and Opinion in the United States,* seems the antitype of James and Dewey, yet what grounded them all was something that derived from Hegelianism. Hegel's incessantly productive World-Spirit, justifying anything and everything through the immanent energies of its dialectical progression, became diluted into a loose cluster of absolute presuppositions: the pre-eminent value of activity, striving, "growth"—the latter a Dewey keynote; a gaseous pervasion of forward-sounding enterprise. It is no wonder that Santayana edged himself toward the side-lines, then left Harvard and America as soon as circumstances allowed. Later on, from a congenial distance on the continent of Europe, he could be shrewdly kind or blandly discriminating about it all, as passages in his *Letters* as well as *Character and Opinion in the United States* show. On the spot it had been stifling:

> What riches have you that you deem me poor,
> Or what large comfort that you call me sad?
> Tell me what makes you so exceeding glad:
> Is your earth happy or your heaven sure?
> I hope for heaven, since the stars endure
> And bring such tidings as our father had.
> I know no deeper doubt to make me mad,
> I need no brighter love to keep me pure.
> To me the faiths of old are daily bread;
> I bless their hope, I bless their will to save,
> And my deep heart still meaneth what they said.
> It makes me happy that the soul is brave,
> And, being so much kinsman to the dead,
> I walk contented to the peopled grave. [69]

Santayana had no special attachment to the present or the future as transient phases of the material flux, and he rather despised the modern spirit blinded by the passions of both. In the religion of the past, especially the traditional Catholic religion of Europe, he revered its piety toward a power "not ourselves," though he did not think such power made for righteousness; and he admired the consecration of spirit that yearned for the perfections which earthly life never realises. "And my deep heart still meaneth what they said." One of Santayana's early poems was about Avila. He knew that the place was basically "sad," as he put it in *Persons and Places,* but the town was a symbol that existence is beautiful only if it is endured with dignity and looks with love toward the farther shore:

> For here hath mortal life from age to age
> Endured the silent hand that makes and mars.
> And, sighing, taken up its heritage
> Beneath the smiling and inhuman stars.
>
> Still o'er this town the crested castle stands,
> A nest for storks, as once for haughty souls,
> Still from the abbey, where the vale expands,
> The curfew for the long departed tolls,
>
> Wafting some ghostly blessing to the heart
> From prayer of nun or silent Capuchin,
> To heal with balm of Golgotha the smart
> Of weary labour and distracted sin.[70]

Yet—in a turn reminiscent of Arnold's "Stanzas from the Grande Chartreuse"—the note of Stoic solitude and self-sufficiency recurs:

> Abroad a tumult, and a ruin here:
> Nor world nor desert hath a home for thee.
> Out of the sorrows of the barren year
> Build thou thy dwelling in eternity.[71]

The fortitude of the solitary spirit, rightly felt to be a markedly Spanish trait in Santayana, must of course be qualified as devoid of any mystical faith in another and higher sphere of existence. Nevertheless the encompassing Realm of Matter on which we all depend, and to whose existence our animal faith testifies, was for Santayana's heterodox spirit almost as profound an object of fearful veneration as God was for the more orthodox type of Spanish soul. There, in that Realm of Matter, lay "the authority of *things*." In such a setting of dogmatic materialism and ultimate irrationalism the ideas that the human mind spins feature merely as the chance expressions of varied organic dispositions. In the next chapter we shall see what an elaborate structure of ideas Santayana in his later philosophical synthesis managed to erect upon such an apparently discouraging basis, drawing into his dialectical web so much of the most exalted spiritual wisdom of the ages. But just as a spider's web is a structure of exquisite refinement and tenacity but suspended across a void, so the dialectical constructions of the human mind are spun as bulwarks of its native aspirations and express merely movements in matter that are shifting, arbitrary, and unknown. In some people, as Santayana put it, "nature lets out this secret." He was one of them, and measured utterance like this makes us feel the chilling resignation entailed by a truly radical disillusion:

I confess that the life of the spider, or my own life, is not one which, if I look at it as a whole, seems to me worth realising; and to say that God's ways are not our ways, and that human tastes and scruples are impertinent, is simply to perceive that moral values cannot preside over nature, and that what arises is not the good, in any prior or absolute sense, but only the possible at that juncture: a natural growth which as it takes form becomes a good in its own eyes, or in the eyes of a sympathetic poet. Then this good realised endows with a relative and retrospective excellence all the conditions favourable to its being, as if with prophetic kindness and parental devotion they had conspired to produce it. The spider is a marvel of pertinacity, and I am not without affection for my own arts and ideas; we both of us heartily welcome the occasions for our natural activities; but when those occasions and activities have passed away, they will not be missed.[72]

·3·

The World and the Spirit:
Later Writings

W. H. AUDEN says somewhere that most people like the smell of their own farts. Santayana, had he not been rather prim, might have said something similar about their liking for their own ideas. Ideas were for him emanations of the body, and all verbal discourse an expression of the physical forces latent beneath the surface of consciousness. The terms of such discourse, which Santayana in his curious nominalistic brand of Platonism called "essences," are always available in a purely logical realm where each is minutely discriminated and eternally self-identical; but when summoned by the existing consciousness of a living organism, they become the expressions of that organism's needs and dispositions: "In seizing upon any particular essence first, discourse is guided by an irrational fatality. Some chance bit is what first occurs to the mind: I run up against this or that, for no logical reason."[1] "Our thoughts—which we may be said to know well, in that we know we have had them often before—are about anything and everything. We shuffle and iterate them, and live in them a verbal, heated, histrionic life. Yet we little know *why* we have them, or how they arise and change."[2] Within this fundamental irrationality discourse spins a web of coherence appropriate to the organic dispositions of the person or group concerned: "Language, in making recognisable sounds to mark similar accidents, tends to cast a net of grammatical relations over the flux of experience, and superposes in this way a partially intelligible syntax on the natural order of genesis in the world."[3] Human consciousness is "a commentary on events in the language of essence; and while its light is contemplative, its movement and intent strictly obey the life of the psyche in which it is kindled."[4]

"Psyche" was the name given in antiquity to the organising principle of matter in living beings, and Santayana retained the term. "There is in every man a Psyche, or inherited nucleus of life, which from its dormant seminal conditions expands and awakes anew in each generation, becoming the person recognised in history, law and morals."[5] He says,

> The Psyche's first care is to surround itself with outer organs like a spider with its web. . . . All the senses, instincts and passions are her scouts. . . . The Psyche, being essentially a way of living, a sort of animated code of hygiene and morals, is a very selective principle: She is perpetually distinguishing—in action if not in words—between good and bad, right and wrong.[6]

In that last passage Santayana characteristically smooths over the fissure between biological and moral existence by means of imagery rather than argument. All that we call "good" is determined by the innate direction of a given physical seed, whether it be that of a species or an individual.

Santayana on several occasions reverts to the image of a spider for evoking the nature of the psyche. The psyche is continually engaged in defensive adaptations to its environment, "torturing itself and uprooting itself from its primary datum."[7] Seldom is it that we live in the pure, undistracted awareness of a datum of consciousness; to live thus is fundamentally what Santayana meant by living spiritually in the Realm of Essence, and we shall dwell at a later stage in this chapter on the images of ascent, illumination, and self-enclosedness that abound in the last volume of *Realms of Being* to express that disposition of the self. For the most part, however, the surrounding world, with its myriad other parcels of animated matter, solicits and engages us. Hence—again the infra-rational image—"suspense outward, towards an object not within her organism, is habitual to the psyche. Her tentacles and her actions hang and grope in mid-air like a drawbridge confidently let down to meet its appropriate ulterior point of contact and support."[8] The energies of the psyche being like tentacles, they weave intricate structures that are an expression of what is latent in her seed as well as protective adaptations against a hostile environment: "A very potent psyche should have entrenched herself in the seed and should surround it later with outworks so staunch and perfect that no ordinary hazard will pierce or bend them."[9] Words and ideas are part of these outworks in human life. It is difficult on momentous topics to bend people by argument. It is their life, not their reason, being addressed.

A spider's web, tentacles, outworks—that is the imagery Santayana used to render his sense of the predicament of the psyche, who at bottom is "a burden to herself, a terrible inner compulsion to care, to watch, to pursue and to possess."[10] "Society is a web of merciless ambitions and jealousies, mitigated by a quite subsidiary kindness . . . human life is precarious, and its only weapon against circumstances, and against rival men, is intelligent action, intelligent war."[11] Yet though existence for a living being is a constant defensive interplay with other beings that are in external relations to itself, the synthesising gift of consciousness may on occasion offer some kind of respite and fulfilment: "In consciousness the psyche becomes festive, lyrical, rhetorical; she caps her life by considering it, and talking to herself about the absent parts of it."[12]

Here at last we glimpse the kind of role philosophy will have in such a vision of existence:

The Psyche, having organised the vital functions of the human animal, begins to ask itself what it is living for. The answer is not, as an unspiritual philosophy would have it: In order to live on. The true answer is: In order to understand, in order to see the Ideas. Those Ideas which the Psyche is able and predestined to discern are such as are illustrated or suggested by its own life, or by the aspects which nature presents to it. Each Idea will be the ideal of something with which the Psyche is naturally conversant; but the good of all these psychic labours will be precisely in clarifying and realising that ideal. . . . The whole of natural life, then, is an aspiration after the realisation and vision of Ideas, and all action is for the sake of contemplation.[13]

Nevertheless the ideal goods in whose contemplation consciousness may repose are the expressions of latent tendencies in given organisms since "the character of the ideas occurring to a man is due to his own character, their action to his action: and the effects said to be produced in the world by an idea flow from the causes by which the idea was itself produced."[14] Recalling again a passage from Santayana's autobiography quoted earlier, we realise that its stark irrationalism was no casual effect:

> My philosophy has never changed. It is by no means an artificial academic hypothesis; it doesn't appeal at all to the professors; it is a system of presuppositions and categories discovered already alive and at work within me, willy-nilly, like existence itself, and virtually present not only in the boy but in the embryo.[15]

Santayana was not the kind of thinker, like the Freudian or the Marxist, who diagnoses irrational factors in the operations of conscious reason only to effect the transition to a mythology of his own, offered as a deeper or more scientific reason. When he claimed that his philosophy was virtually present in the embryo, he meant exactly what he said. It was that little seed which sprouted in the philosophical systems of *The Life of Reason* and *Realms of Being,* and it was justified not as truth, but as the powerfully integrated expression of an organic disposition. This may appear a surrender of any claim to be seriously philosophical, yet there are hints that have some bearing on it in other modern philosophers, whenever they suggest that there is an alternative to viewing philosophy as the handmaiden of the physical sciences, or as purely logical analysis.

Isaiah Berlin, for instance, has written that the task of the philosopher is to examine the conflict between various modes of discourse "with a view to constructing other, less internally contradictory, less pervertible metaphors, images, symbols and systems of categories."[16] This allusion to metaphor and symbol posits a flexibility that does not view philosophy according to a single truth-bearing model, and may therefore suggest an understanding of Santayana. Nevertheless, it still sees philosophy as helping to implement the gradual rational progress of mankind. It is an Enlightenment view, and as such it does not catch the note of Santayana. Similar to it, but more helpful perhaps for placing him, is the view of F. C. Copleston when discussing the phenomenological approach to philosophy. Without precisely demonstrating anything in a strict logical sense, or arriving at a set of testable conclusions, such an approach is valuable, Copleston tells us, in "drawing attention" to aspects of experience with the aid of metaphor and imagery and in achieving a change of direction in the "focussing of attention."[17] This way of looking at philosophy may remind us in turn of the essay in which Friedrich Waismann, a close associate of Wittgenstein in the latter's final years, takes issue with the whole notion of demonstration or proof having any real role in philosophy: "Philosophical arguments don't prove anything. Yet they have force." This sounds promising, since, whatever the shortcomings of Santayana's mature philosophy, it has extraordinary rhetorical power—"force"—in propounding a view of man's situation in the world: a weltanschauung. And Waismann, a little later in the same essay, isolates what he considers to be the essential of philosophy in one word: vision. Yet he hastens to add that he "does not wish to romanticise what he means." Thereupon, in a manner resembling Isaiah Berlin, he goes on to speak of philosophy "breaking fetters," "piercing" the dead crust of convention and tradition, so as to attain "a new and broader way of looking at things."[18] Ironically enough, Santayana would have called such terminology thoroughly romantic. Let us call it rather the terminology of the Enlightenment. For all its accommodating factors, it still carries the strong suggestion that philosophy is a process of clarifying problems with a view to dispelling ignorance and banishing retrograde attitudes. Santayana remains unassimilable.

Van Meter Ames has a pleasant anecdote when reminiscing about his meetings with Santayana in Rome in the 1930s. Santayana told him that "intellectual work was not a burden for him"—Waismann wouldn't have liked that!—and "it's no trouble for me to think because I think only of what occurs to me. If I had a problem to solve, that would be terrible."[19] Even if we allow for the element of calculated impishness, Santayana has surely touched on something important here. It is what led Desmond Macarthy to make a remark about the experience of reading him that many others must have felt; as one turns his pages one may be full of admiration, even dazzlement, but one is little tempted to argue with him: "As a rule I quarrel and wrangle with philosophers readily enough. Why have I argued so little with Mr. Santayana?" Macarthy goes on:

There is (and I imagine I am expressing what many have felt) a quality in his writings which induces passivity in his readers. He is so suavely sure of himself, so elegantly and sympathetically dogmatic, so indulgent to the prejudice of others, so frank in calmly maintaining his own, that it seems crude to ask him sharply what it all comes to. He is so round a man. You have a soothing and, at the same time, a subduing impression that he understands where the difference between you and him lies better than you do yourself, and that he has allowed for such differences long, long ago. Presently he will explain your temperament from which they sprang. You may jerk and jump a little while in the net, not of his logic, but of his sympathetic sagacity, yet presently you lie passive in it, dumb as a fish drawn up from its own element into one more rarefied; and there, with ever more gently panting gills, the restless intellect at last gives up its wilful breath. It is a delicious euthanasia. When I read Mr. Santayana I find myself murmuring, with an irony I can hardly fathom, the last words of that Roman Emperor who, on his deathbed, said: "I suppose I am becoming a god." But, the book closed, I discover myself to have become no such thing. I cannot even remember how wise I lately was, or why I felt so wise.[20]

That is a passage of feline dissection worthy of Santayana himself. Macarthy wrote it at the beginning of his review of *Soliloquies in England,* exquisitely ruminative short pieces by Santayana, some of which show a tinge of resemblance to the mood of Renan or Anatole France, with all that this implies of rather cloying *homme du monde* wisdom. The urgent eloquence of *Realms of Being* and other later writings is occasionally lacking. Yet Macarthy, who went on to write an admiring critique of *Soliloquies in England,* has in suitably provocative fashion alerted us to how far Santayana's way of writing is from the expected effect of philosophical discourse, even though it deals with many traditional philosophical "problems" and shows no mean dialectical skill at times in offering "solutions" to such problems. We come nearer to an angle of vision appropriate to Santayana in a comment John Holloway made about his approach to the Victorian Sage, in his book of that name. He wrote of the crucial effect of figurative language in the work of his subjects, who were undoubtedly thinkers, but whose power seemed to lie in conveying "single total impressions"[21] on the reader, by cumulative effects of imagery and tonal virtuosity. And this will remind us again of the primary intuition that Bergson held to be implicit in a philosophical system, and of the mediating images that it generates or implies.

William James records that an early essay of Santayana struck the Harvard Philosophy Department as "a little too much like a poem."[22] His writings never ceased to impress unsympathetic critics in that way, even when he provided an elaborate bony structure from traditional metaphysics of the essence-existence type in order to convey his innate disposition toward the world. Near the end of his life, he wrote to a young man who had been trying respectfully to elicit from him a more full-blooded response to the absolute rightness of the democratic ideals that had recently triumphed in the Second World War:

> Argument has never been, in my opinion, a good method in philosophy, because I feel real misunderstanding or difference in sentiment usually rests on hidden presuppositions or limitations that are irreconcilable, so that the superficial war of words irritates without leading to any agreement. . . . In your difficulty with my way of putting things I suspect that there is less technical divergence between us than divergence in outlook upon the world.[23]

And to all the acute minds who had chewed over his doctrines in a festschrift volume of essays in 1940 he urbanely showed the door in the following words: "I am a scholastic only in my principles, not in my ways. I detest disputation and distrust proofs and disproofs. . . . I send my critics back to their respective camps with my blessing, hoping that the world may prove staunch and beautiful to them, pictured in their own terms."[24]

"Pictured in their own terms"—philosophical systems are viewed as expressions of temperament. In a late autobiographical piece, entitled "The Idler and His Works," Santayana was even more candid about what he called his "meanderings." What he meant by the word was not primarily the rhetorical diffuseness of his writings, but the way in which he had got side-tracked in his earlier career by adventitious problems and arguments not central to the intellectual vista that fortune had predestined him to reveal; and he claimed as an achievement what many philosophers see as a flaw. He had gradually managed to "infuse more and more of myself into the apprehension of the world and of its opinions, until in 'Realms of Being' the picture of them becomes itself a confession and an image of the mind that composed it."[25] This invites us to turn once again to a revealing passage in Santayana's autobiography, where in old age he illuminated the nature of his weltanschauung by conveying the emotional kernel from which his work sprang.

When Santayana was five years old, he tells us in *Persons and Places,* his mother left him for three years in Spain with his father and his father's family, while she along with his two half-sisters joined his half-brother in Boston so as to be near their Sturgis relatives. The dry detachment of the aged Santayana gives added pungency to the narrating of a nightmarish time. The family squabbled abominably. A young cousin lost her baby in great agony and died in the house they all inhabited at Avila. His uncle, Santiago, slowly went off his head. "This crowded, strained, disunited and tragic family life remains for me the type of what life really is: something confused, hideous and useless." The uncle, Santiago, far gone in drink and worn down by the trials of his existence, would ceaselessly walk round, half singing, half moaning, always repeating the same sounds and crushing a piece of paper in his hand: "He had recovered the animal capacity—such an insult to the world!—of still doing his old trick, no matter what might be going on. The marvel is how many individuals and how many governments are able to survive on this system. Perhaps the universe is nothing but an equilibrium of idiocies."

Flanked by those evocations of primeval family chaos is a description of his young cousin's baby, born dead after much pain. The six-year-old Santayana caught a glimpse of it lying in

a small wooden box that might have held soap or candles, a dead child lying naked, pale, yellowish green. Most beautiful, I thought him, and as large and perfectly formed as the Child Jesus in the pictures. . . . The image of that child, as if made of green alabaster, has remained clear all my life, not as a ghastly object that ought to have been hidden from me, but as the most beautiful of statues, something too beautiful to be alive.[26]

Santayana is not aiming at contrived symbolism in those passages. He is simply describing what he remembers. Yet it is difficult not to feel that the juxtaposing of something "too beautiful to be alive" with the chaotic ignominy of what actually was living has an uneasy bearing on something central to Santayana's philosophical vision of existence. Had he not written in the same volume of autobiography that when young he considered "the real was rotten and only the imaginary truly good," and that "allowing for the rash generalizations of youth, it is still what I think"? Such primary responses to existence—visceral, physiological, and consolidating themselves in the obscure certainties of an emotional disposition—probably have more effect on the reasoned judgements of later life than many would be willing to concede. They are worth bearing in mind when considering Santayana's considered philosophical views on matter and existence, as we shall shortly be doing. Freudian interpretations tend to over-rationalise these arcana by mythological schematisms, by what Santayana called "literary psychology." Really it is all a mystery of genetics and biology, and "embryology, the most obscure part of biology, is the fundamental part of it." [27]

Santayana had to concede that the terms of his own evocation of the fundamental nature of existence were also a kind of literary psychology. Such terms, being what he called "essences," cannot be identical with the reality they evoke. Yet he felt that his frankly poetical discourse about the material principle of existence was in its way closer to the heart of things than the attenuated symbolisms of the mathematical physicists, whose achievements through the course of time have gained precision and practical import at the cost of concreteness and vital cogency. They are all "too graphic and mathematical," and "the persistence of substance can hardly be intrinsically similar to some ghostly image": [28]

Weight and figure are not more characteristic of matter than are explosiveness, swiftness, fertility, and radiation. Planters and breeders of animals, or poets watching the passing generations of mankind, will feel that the heart and mystery of matter lie in the seeds of things, *semina rerum,* and in the customary cycles of their transformation. It is by its motion and energy, by its fidelity to measure and law, that matter has become the substance of our world, and the principle of life and of death in it. The earliest sages, no less than the latest moderns, identified matter with fire, aether, or fluids, rather than with stocks and stones;

the latter are but temporary concretions, and always in the act of growing or crumbling. Even those who, partly for dialectical reasons, reduced matter to impenetrable atoms, attributed all its fertility to the play of collisions which swept perpetually through the void and drove those dead atoms into constellations and vortices and organisms. This endless propulsion and these fated complications were no less material, and far more terrible, than any monumental heap into which matter might sometimes be gathered, and which to a gaping mind might seem more substantial. If any poet ever felt the life of nature in its truth, irrepressible, many-sided, here flaming up savagely, there helplessly dying down, that poet was Lucretius, whose materialism was unqualified.[29]

Terrible, irrepressible, savage and yet helpless—those glosses by Santayana on the Lucretian response to the material substance of all things tell us perhaps more about the modern poet-philosopher than about his ancient mentor. Santayana's language is particularly highly charged on this topic; a horror akin to the Gnostic or the Manichean seems to take possession of him as he dwells on the power of the dark mother of all things. Let us assemble a composite impression by culling brief passages almost at random from *Scepticism and Animal Faith* and *Realms of Being*. (I shall italicise phrases that seem particularly striking in their emotive quality.)

Matter, not spirit, is the seat and principle of the flux . . . in respect to the realm of matter, spirit is like a child asking questions, and making pause, and often *brutally run over and crushed by a rush of changes which it cannot understand.*[30]

In deliberate decisions and actions, the spirit may feel the rising tide in the psyche surging in this and that direction, till it bursts into some clear idea or word or deed; but that whole process went on *in the dark, in the bowels of the world of which the psyche is a portion:* and the spirit, in great excitement and perturbation, felt those alternatives and decisions of the Will, sometimes with joy, sometimes with horror: for Will is often like wave in Racine, and *recoils aghast at the monster it has vomited.*[31]

The world is as evil for the natural Will as the natural Will is evil for the world. *The true sin is cosmic and constitutional;* it is the heritage of Chaos. This is the sin of which spirit is the innocent victim.[32]

Microbes devour no less efficaciously than wild beasts; and this *perpetual inner waste,* met by the need of replenishment, is the clearest of demonstrations that matter is the principle of existence. *Matter is essentially food, an object of competition* and a substance fit for assimilation. It is forever withdrawing itself from one form and assuming another, or being redigested. . . . Every living being must feed, feed perpetually, or it dissolves . . . *the horrid simultaneity of eating and being eaten.*[33]

Existence is no spectacle, though spectacles and calculations may amuse or describe it. In ourselves and in the objects on our own plane encountered in action, *existence is a strain and an incubus, particular, self-centered, substantial.* It is in terms of such existence, unstable but burdened and concrete, that an unsophisticated natural philosophy might conceive the realm of matter.[34]

The Prayer Book thanks God for our creation; yet in being created we received nothing but needs with no assurance that they would be satisfied: *for what is our organic Will, our psyche, but a vast concourse of needs, some urgent, others latent but brewing and rendering us fundamentally unhappy?*[35]

The sense of existence evidently belongs to the intoxication, to the *Rausch* of existence itself; it is *the strain of life within me,* prior to all intuition, *that in its precipitation and terror,* passing as it continually must from one untenable condition to another, stretches my attention absurdly over what is not given, over the lost and unattained, the before and after which are wrapped in darkness, and confuses my breathless apprehension of the clear presence of all I can ever truly behold.[36]

The whole life of imagination and knowledge comes from within, from *the restlessness, eagerness, curiosity and terror of the animal bent on hunting, feeding and breeding;* and the throb of being which he experiences at any moment is not proper to the datum in his mind's eye—a purely fantastic essence—but to himself. It is out of his organism or its central part, the psyche, that this datum has been bred. The living substance within being bent, in the first instance, on pursuing and avoiding some agency in its environment, it projects whatever (in consequence of its reactions) reaches its consciousness into the locus whence it finds the stimulus to come, and thus it frames its description or knowledge of objects. In this way the ego really and sagaciously posits the non-ego; not absolutely, as Fichte imagined, not by a gratuitous fiat, but on occasion and for the best of reasons, when the *non-ego in its might shakes the ego out of its primitive somnolence.*[37]

To be startled is to be aware that something sudden and mysterious has occurred not far from me in space. The thunder-clap is felt to be an event in the self and in the not-self, even before its nature as a sound— its aesthetic quality for the self—is recognised at all; I first know *I am shaken horribly,* and then note how loud and rumbling is the voice of the god that shakes me. That *first feeling of something violent and resistless happening in the world at large,* is accompanied by a hardly less primitive sense of something gently seething within me, a smouldering fire which that alien energy blows upon and causes to start into life.[38]

The radical stuff of experience is breathlessness, or pulsation, or as Locke said (correcting himself) *a certain uneasiness;* a lingering thrill, the resonance of that much-struck bell which I call my body, *the continual assault of some masked enemy. . . .* The first thing experience reports is the existence of something, merely *as existence, the weight, strain, danger and lapse of being.*[39]

Disregarding the epistemological problems that arise from such passages (and there are many more such in Santayana's later writings), their cumulative effect is impressive simply as a phenomenology of alienation. Man is an animal in the dark, blown upon and buffeted, feeding and fighting, frightened and aggressive, his psyche an inherent element of the fertile darkness that both uses and destroys it. Consciousness, spirit, is a flickering light, for the most part purely instrumental as it seizes upon essences that express its tactical relationship with the outer world, but fleetingly capable of contemplative absorption in those essences. There only lies its fulfilment. We shall attend to this redemptive factor in Santayana's philosophy at a later stage.

Before doing so, we must dwell on another factor mitigating his rather appalling metaphysical sentiment concerning the fundamental nature of being. In his later writings he could hardly have sustained a discriminating concern with cultural forms had he remained wholly absorbed in the dazzling darkness of existential chaos, like some latter-day Lucretius of the Absurd. At the conclusion of the chapter of *Scepticism and Animal Faith* from which our very last extract came, another note was struck, and to it we must now give heed:

I am a sensitive creature surrounded by a universe utterly out of scale with myself: I must, therefore, address it questioningly but trustfully, and it must reply to me in my own terms, in symbols and parables, that only gradually enlarge my childish perceptions. It is as if Substance said to Knowledge: My child, there is a great world for thee to conquer, but it is a vast, an ancient, and a recalcitrant world. It yields wonderful treasures to courage, when courage is guided by art and respects the limits set to it by nature. I should not have been so cruel as to give thee birth, if there had been nothing for thee to master; but having first prepared the field, I set in thy heart the love of adventure.[40]

All is not totally dark. Civilisations have existed and continue to do so. Chaos is manageable in part, the psyche ingenious and adaptable. Matter is not just a predicament for consciousness; it is also an opportunity, if man correctly divines the direction of its flow, and if the conventions evolved are not too grossly at variance with what circumstances permit. There are in matter what Santayana called "tropes," rhythms of recurrence that human arts may turn to advantage. An organised way of life emerges and creates through language and symbolism as well as through crafts and industries a settled mode of existence. The existence of anything definite, coherent, and sustained always impressed Santayana as evidence of a powerful harmonising impulse at work in the psyche, so that he was led to remark at one point that "only an orthodoxy can possibly be right, as against the bevy of its heresies, which represent wayward exclusion, or a fundamental disloyalty." He added, however, that

no orthodoxy can be right as against another orthodoxy, if this expresses an equal sensitiveness to the facts within its purview and an equal intellectual power. All values are moral and consistency is but a form of honour and courage. It marks singleness of purpose and the pressure of the total reality upon an earnest mind, capable of recollection.[41]

Singleness of purpose betokens a powerful impulse toward integration of form and definition of character. In Santayana a marked responsiveness to underlying chaos and pervasive flux was balanced by an equal responsiveness to any powerfully integrated form expressing a triumphant vital adaptation to circumstances. In an early work like *The Life of Reason,* such aestheticism was qualified by liberal and progressive overtones. The latter faded as he grew older so that he could write to his sister, even as early as 1910, "I sympathise with the self preserving instinct of formed things rather than with the destructive forces of nature, such as democratic envy, fury and ignorance are."[42] Even more comprehensively dismissive was a later passage from the Preface to *Dominations and Powers,* where he writes that his own sympathies

go out to harmony in strength, no matter how short-lived. The triumph of life lies in achieving perfection of form; and the richer and more complex the organism is that attains this perfection, the more glorious its perfection will be and the more unstable. Longevity is a vulgar good, and vain after all when compared with eternity. It is the privilege of the dust and the lowest and most primitive organisms. The gods love and keep in their memories the rare beauties that die young. I prefer the rose to the dandelion; I prefer the lion to the vermin in the lion's skin. In order to obtain anything lovely I would gladly extirpate all the crawling ugliness in the world.[43]

The integrity of an achieved form is also a natural and legitimate principle of exclusion. Santayana deplored the nineteenth-century ideal of peace that had to be bought at the cost of eliminating distinctive traditions and spreading industrial benefits within a framework of levelling tolerance, which is only a covert form of domination. "Between two nothings there is eternal peace: but between two somethings, if they come within range of each other, there is always danger of war."[44] A resemblance to Santayana's point of view appears from an unexpected quarter. Nadezhda Mandelstam tells us that in his earlier years her husband, too, was repelled by the poverty of nineteenth-century liberal ideals in which he "did not see the harmony and grandeur he wanted." He wanted a society with a "clearly defined structure," and he sensed the presence in both Marxism and Catholicism of "a unifying idea that bound the whole structure together. . . . For this reason he was not frightened by the idea of authority, even when it was translated into dictatorial power."[45] Mandelstam was doomed to regret those likings. Santayana, too, was not averse to dictators, since he believed in principle that a single directive will intelligently representative of the true interests of a given people was an ideal form of government, as we see from his essay "Ideal Monarchy" in *Dominations and Powers.* By a fortunate providence Santayana remained personally insulated from the practical implications of his aesthetic authoritarianism within the happily unperfected tyranny of Mussolini's Italy. His views on these matters remained on record, however, and led him to some disconcerting utterances.

In the 1930s, Santayana exchanged letters with Sydney Hook, then in his Marxist phase. He told Hook that

I am not a conservative in the sense of being afraid of revolutions, like Hobbes, or thinking order, *in the sense of peace,* the highest good; and I am not at all attached to things as they are, or as they were in my youth. But I love order in the sense of organised, harmonious, consecrated living: and for this reason I sympathise with the Soviets and Fascists and the Catholics, but not at all with the liberals. I should sympathise with the Nazis too, if their system were, even in theory, founded on reality; but it is Nietzschean, founded on Will: and therefore a sort of romanticism gone mad, rather than a serious organisation of material forces—which would be the only way, I think, of securing moral coherence. . . . I hope that (the Soviets) may succeed in establishing a great new order of society, definite, traditional and self-justified.[46]

The latter pious wish has come true, but hardly in a form with which one feels Santayana would have had much sympathy. Later he qualified his views on Communism, but still managed to get a side-swipe at the liberals: "The same nominal humanitarianism, inwardly contradicted by a militant hatred towards almost all human institutions and affections, has descended from the wealth-loving liberals to the poverty-hating communists."[47] And in a telling sentence about the Marxists in the final volume of his autobiography, he remarked: "Merciless irrational ambition has borrowed the language of brotherly love."[48] Santayana had considerable respect for Marxist materialism as a good working hypothesis in historical investigation but no respect at all for "dialectical" materialism, which was Jewish messianism drunk on logic.

After the Second World War he changed his tune about the Fascists and the Nazis. He judged their impetus to have

failed before the massive resistance of a less trained, more humane, more deeply rooted civilisation. It was by no means to the jungle that

Fascism and Nazism wished to reduce the world, but on the contrary to an engineer's and school master's ideal of rigid and universal order. All the wanton branches of the human tree were to be cut off in order that one vertical stem should flourish in solitary perfection.[49]

Santayana acknowledges here that the diversity permitted by liberalism, when it is not just deviously attempting a hegemony of its own, is closer to his own ideal of a variety of vital orders than the single "coherence" and "integrity" fostered by Fascism, Nazism and, by implication, Communism. Nevertheless a conflict between Santayana's urbanely inflexible relativism and the universalist outlook of Western liberal democracy must always be latent, and it emerged in an engaging series of letters after the Second World War between the sage and a young American philosopher, John Yolton.

Yolton, conscious that his country had been triumphant in what he took to be an absolutely just cause, was anxious to square such justice with the relativistic views of a thinker whom he clearly admired. Surely, he wrote, "the imposition of some sort of moral 'ought' upon all societies seems to be required by the present world situation." And surely, he added, the ideal of international government that Santayana himself had advanced in one chapter of *Dominations and Powers* was "more than just a description" on Santayana's part.

Santayana would have none of it. Courteously, as always, but with extreme firmness, he denied any attachment to the view that "it is a moral aspiration or predestination that rules the world and that our efforts can accelerate that consummation."[50] Government is justified and good if it authentically expresses a harmony between intelligent will and opportune circumstances. For some political systems, the authentic good consists in being militant and in aiming at universal domination. There are no absolutes. As he put it in *Dominations and Powers,* "The same government that is a benign and useful power for one class or one province may exercise a cruel domination over another province or another class." It is all a play of irrational and unpredictable forces:

What a man lives for is hardly better known to a man, or less often falsely described in orations, than what the government works for.

These are, for both, incidental successes and failures, clearly distinguishable, but ultimate aims are not discerned, for the excellent reason that they do not exist. The generative order of society proceeds not towards an ultimate good but by a concourse of tentative actions, each more or less expressing a particular need, passion, or purpose; and the total issue is a compound of clashing endeavours, and chequered fortunes.[51]

Goethe's Mephistopheles made a rather similar point:

> O weh! Hinweg! und lass mir jene Streite
> Von Tyrannei und Sklaverei beiseite!
> Mich langweilt's: denn kaum ist's abgetan,
> So fangen sie von vorne wieder an;
> Und keiner merkt: er ist doch nur geneckt
> Von Asmodeus, der dahinter steckt.
> Sie streifen sich, so heisst's, um Freiheitsrechte;
> Genau besehn, sind's Knechte gegen Knechte.[52]

> Oh! Cut it out! You can ignore for me
> These broils of tyranny and slavery!
> It bores me; for their war is hardly done
> Before another war must be begun;
> And no-one sees himself a marionette
> Who's teased by Asmodeus behind the set.
> They say they're fighting for the rights of freedom—
> Slave against slave, should you more truly heed 'em.

Such views, though they may shock—they clearly shocked Yolton—are consistent with Santayana's primary intuition concerning the psyche and its dependence on material forces that envelop it and generate its preferences. And, being consistent, they must be true, in the sense of expressing the integrity of Santayana's organic disposition. The circle is impermeable by any other type of reasoning, because reason for Santayana was at best a harmony among the passions and not an ideal destined to govern the passions by virtue of emanating from a superior source, be it God, History, Natural Law, or Conscience. It is true that he had advanced a tentative scheme of rational world government in *Dominations and Powers,* involving a central economic authority that would allow complete autonomy to the customs and traditions of the separate moral societies we call nations; but he had done so "playfully," as he himself put it, as a Utopian exercise. This was a sign, he smoothly informed Yolton, of "how different his Weltanschauung was from that of modern politicians." [53] Yolton, who later wrote with sympathetic shrewdness on Santayana, was on this occasion trumped.

Christopher Isherwood, in a review of *Dominations and Powers* nicely blending mockery with admiration, put his finger on a quality of Santayana's political views that bears on the exchange of letters with Yolton. These views reminded him, Isherwood wrote, of a Zen koan, when a pupil is presented by his spiritual mentor with some seemingly nonsensical question: "Suppose you have a duck in a bottle; how will you get it out without breaking the bottle or hurting the duck?"

The pupil attempts to give a rational answer to this question, finds that he cannot, and is thereby reduced to a state of acute intellectual agony verging on madness, from which, it is claimed, he is sometimes released by a flash of intuitive enlightenment. Suddenly, he understands, in some non-rational manner, that his dilemma is unreal. The duck-bottle relationship is not fundamental. It is only a symbol of an imaginary bondage in which we live and from which we could free ourselves at any moment.

Dominations and Powers seems to me to be a sort of political *koan*. Santayana's ambiguity, his frivolous proposals, his self-contradictions and his maddening style all combine to drive us into the mood of desperation experienced by the Zen pupil. . . .

. . . Doesn't he, in presenting us with all these irreconcilable opposites, these irresistible Dominations opposed to immovable Powers, slyly endeavour to make us transcend them? Isn't he really trying to show us that the only true solution of our problems is to be found in a refusal of all solutions? How else, in the presence of our contemporary disaster, could he sit there in his study and smile? [54]

Santayana would have smiled in the presence of any disaster, contemporary or otherwise. How could one imagine that existence is anything but a mitigated disaster? True, there may be conservative societies like the Avila of his youth, [55] where custom has moulded character to a certain resigned dignity; but "spirit has no wish and no power to establish permanent things or persons or types in the world; that is the world's business, if it cares to be conservative, as it must be up to a certain point if it is to rise at all out of chaos, yet as it can never be altogether, since it has chaos in its heart."[56] Liberals, the companions and harbingers of chaos for Santayana, abounding in humanitarian zealotry and prosperous greed, exhibited a more perverse brand of domination than most others. They restlessly undermine such fragile stabilities and continuities as exist for the sake of phantasmal future good: "Liberals and Pacifists, who imagine they represent morality in general, are the first to announce the sure victory of their cause and the annihilation for ever of all their enemies, that is, of all moralities in particular."[57] There is, however, a way out of the jungle of competing wills, and Isherwood neatly and amusingly directed us to this feature of Santayana.

Isherwood rightly sensed that a work like *Dominations and Powers,* Santayana's most extended consideration of politics and society in his later writings, and a counterpoise to much of the earlier *Life of Reason,* was in essence a kind of shadow-boxing. Santayana did not really take the social arena seriously any longer as a source of salvation. Of course a society can be more or less valued according to the way it fosters the liberal arts and the joys of contemplation. Those are its "Virtues," as Santayana put it in the first chapter of his late treatise on politics, as distinct from the "Dominations" and "Powers" that within a single society, and among societies at large, enact a constant struggle between shifting and incompatible types of good. As a result, harmony, Santayana's hold-all word for the good in his earlier as in his later writings, shifts the context of its possible realisation from the outer to the inner sphere. There is always, of course, a hint in Santayana that traditional societies are likely to be less distracting to the spirit than other kinds. But they, too, are earthly cities:

Human society, in principle, is but another ant-hill: it clings and grows on the earth's surface like moss on the rocks; its passions, its maxims, its interests are variations on the ferocious or diligent habits of other animals. Language and science take the place among us of the instincts, to us incomprehensible, that govern insects and birds in their vital economy. Religion itself, when established in society, is for the spirit only a part of the world. It perplexes, it constrains, it deceives like all those other pompous institutions by which the world carries on its merciless business. Merciless, casual, blind this whole engine of existence certainly is: yet where anything is allowed for a time to run smoothly or bask peacefully or move grandly, beauty and joy radiate from it to the delight of the spirit, which itself radiates, when it can, from the core of life, to observe and to celebrate all that surrounds it.[58]

Radiation from the core of life means radiation from the individual psyche. Political societies, though they may achieve more or less of stability, serenity, and integrity of purpose, are not truly organisms. Santayana never fell headlong into that particular trap of the conservative theorist, though he may occasionally have hovered on the edge of it.

Society is not an organism at the same level as living individuals that nature reproduces from seeds and endows with political consciousness. . . . Every member of a society wears his loyalties like a garment, which decency and safety do not allow him to discard; yet he remains naked beneath, a wild man and a traitor in his natural person.[59]

In some anarchic biological sense we may be tempted to call Santayana a liberal, because for him freedom was at the root of things as well as at their zenith. What Hegel disparaged as the abstract or negative freedom of the individual, which should seek fulfilment in the higher consciousness of State or World History, was for Santayana fundamental precisely because unmediated. In his autobiography, having confessed that "the lady who said she envied me for not having a conscience didn't altogether misread me," he proceeded:

Like my mother I have firmness of character; and I don't understand how a rational being can be wrong in being or doing what he fundamentally wishes to be or to do. He may make a mistake about it, or about the circumstances; or he may be imperfectly integrated, and tossed between contrary desires, not knowing his own nature or what he really wants. Experience and philosophy have taught me that perfect integrity is an ideal never fully realized, that nature is fluid and inwardly chaotic in the last resort, even in the most heroic soul; and I am ashamed and truly repentant if ever I find that I have been dazed and false to myself either in my conduct or in my opinions. In this sense I am not without a conscience; but I accept nobody's precepts traversing my moral freedom.[60]

Moral freedom for Santayana lay in detachment from social and political ties, which the free mind must view with "resigned courtesy," [61] and in the ability to live spiritually in what he called the Realm of Essence, which he sharply set off against material existence. The technical essence-existence distinction has already been touched on several times in the course of this book. It was a heritage of scholasticism to which Santayana gave his own peculiar colouring, and with good cause it has greatly exercised his strictly philosophical commentators. We must try to understand its principal features on philosophical terms, and then let it expand a little so as to fortify the view of Santayana being advanced. It will be obvious at the outset that a man whose major philosophical work culminates with long chapters entitled "Distraction," "Liberation," and "Union" is not purely concerned with theoretical distinctions in logic and epistemology. He is in quest of salvation, not of solutions. Santayana's philosophy is a thoroughly practical pursuit, directed toward release from the Wheel in the manner of Buddhists.

His principal enterprise began after the First World War in *Scepticism and Animal Faith,* the introductory volume to *Realms of Being,* its opening chapters a radical epistemological exercise reducing certainty to the mind's intuition of a single datum, or essence: this blue. It was what Santayana called a "solipsism of the present moment." That technical solipsism remains worth bearing in mind, even though Santayana argued himself clear of any final commitment to it and regained contact with the commonsense view of things by his doctrine of animal faith. He was as convinced as G. E. Moore that philosophical scepticism and the idealism into which it can so easily fall was a pose sustained only by intricate sophisms, but he did not hold out his two hands in front of a British Academy audience, as Moore did on a famous occasion, so as to spin a fine web of commonsense views around those two unimpeachable objects. He preferred in *Realms of Being* and *Scepticism and Animal Faith* to evoke by means of imagination and rhetoric a sense of the shock and pressure of that indisputable presence called the "outer world." Nevertheless the choice of a solipsistic starting-point showed a temperamental leaning toward mental isolation and self-containment, and distantly prefigured the spiritual stance attained at the end of *Realms of Being* where the spirit dwells in solitary self-communion with the essences congenial to it. "If belief and anxiety be banished from the experience of things," Santayana wrote, "only its pure essence remains present to the mind."[62]

What I call essence is not something alleged to exist or subsist in some higher sphere: it is the last residuum of scepticism and analysis. Whatsoever existing fact we may think we encounter, there will be obvious features distinguishing that alleged fact from any dissimilar fact and from nothing. All such features, discernible in sense, thought or fancy, are essences; and the realm of essence which they compose is simply the catalogue, infinitely extensible, of all characters logically distinct and ideally possible. Apart from the events they may figure in, these essences have no existence; and since the realm of essence, by definition, is infinitely comprehensive and without bias, it can exercise no control over the existing world, nor determine what features shall occur in events, or in what order.[63]

Essences thus described do not sound very interesting: a rather loose extension of Platonic, Aristotelian, and scholastic doctrines concerning the formal aspect of being, but deprived of all hierarchy and teleology, and sounding as miscellaneous as the data of an empiricist. A good deal of Santayana's elaborate dialectic about the technical implications of his essence-existence distinction in *Realms of Being* and elsewhere reads like a protracted case of the philosophical concept-spinning that J. L. Austin would have delighted to puncture. That was how Santayana tended to express himself when writing with an eye to the metaphysicians who might suspect him of foisting some mystical doctrine about essence on the reading public. Rather different, and far more revealingly characteristic, is a passage such as the following, also from *Scepticism and Animal Faith,* where technical discussion of essence blossoms into rhetorical hyperbole, and one realises that Santayana in his doctrine of essence is not so much offering a theoretical explanation of the nature of things as recommending a quality of attention to things that it is in our power to cultivate, and that, if cultivated, conduce to spiritual peace. His is a scepticism like that of certain Greek thinkers of the Hellenistic period, who doubted all things so as not to be seduced from inner concentration by the distracting solicitations of the outer world:

Since any essence I happen to have hit upon is independent of me and would possess its precise character if I had never been born, or had never been led by the circumstances of my life and temperament to apprehend that particular essence, evidently all other essences, which I have not been led to think of, rejoice in the same sort of impalpable being—impalpable, yet the only sort of being that the most rugged experience can ever actually find. Thus a mind enlightened by scepticism and cured of noisy dogma, a mind discounting all reports, and free from all tormenting anxiety about its own fortunes or existence, finds in the wilderness of essence a very sweet and marvelous solitude. The ultimate reaches of doubt and renunciation open out for it, by an easy transition, into fields of endless variety and peace, as if through the gorges of death it had passed into a paradise where all things are crystallised into the image of themselves, and have lost their urgency and their venom.[64]

"Tormenting anxiety," "noisy dogma," "urgency" and "venom," "gorges of death"—we note again the type of vocabulary that characterises so many of Santayana's evocations of the realm of matter where the anxious human animal finds itself in a state of Heideggerian *Geworfenheit*. For Aristotle, matter was pure unknowable potentiality having no intelligible content, but Santayana, like the Gnostics, was very free with epithets suggesting its alien and hostile nature. In spite of their oracular ring, however, such phrases about matter have, on Santayana's own premises, no strict truth, but at best only a loose symbolic suggestiveness. All that the mind ever knows is essences, and the essences hit upon by one particular animal organism gifted with consciousness to explain its own relation to the world are merely the expressive symbols of its own inner sense of things. Therefore all knowledge for Santayana was imaginative: a "salutation and not an embrace," as he put it. Animal faith, groping through the world with the aid of essences, may find its symbols pragmatically effective, or inwardly consoling, but they are never valid tokens of what material existence is "in itself." Why, one may ask, should it always turn out that essences—let us say the mathematical symbols of the physicist—bear successfully on matter, if it is simply the chance eddies of a material flux that generate the symbolising psyche, with no co-ordinating principle at work in the form of a divine ordering agent or immanent teleology? How does it happen that mental forms mesh so successfully with material being if there is such a fundamental dichotomy in their principles? Furthermore, on Santayana's own materialist premises, it is difficult to justify theoretically the poignant suggestion of the spirit's transcendence of material existence that the fervour of his rhetoric insistently conveys, even though he is careful at other times to make clear that he holds an epiphenomenal view of mind in relation to matter. All such doubts are valid and important, and philosophical critics have expended much high quality ink on Santayana in connection with these problems. But of course, as he told Van Meter Ames, he himself had no "problems." And that *boutade* is worth dwelling on again.

At the risk of seeming in professional eyes to diminish the strictly philosophical arguments of a man who was, after all, a major and respected figure in important technical controversy in the first half of his career, I should say that we understand him best if we view his later writings as an attempt to render the misery of the human condition and a way of overcoming it. And that is not a "problem" in the narrowly philosophical sense. He used traditional terminology because it sometimes bore usefully on an attempt to "bring the whole soul of man into activity" rather than confine the soul to the level of proof and counterproof. Admittedly one doubts whether Coleridge—or Wordsworth—would have approved of the direction of Santayana's sensibility; but a link at least with the Shelley of *Adonais,* or with Leopardi, is arguably more helpful for understanding him than aligning him with austere logicians and metaphysicians. In the Preface he wrote for Iris Origo's book on Leopardi there is a singularly eloquent passage that, while conveying by an image the essence of Leopardi's poetic gift, also gives us a telling example of what Santayana means by the spiritual intuition of essence as a redemptive factor in existence:

The student, the writer, the sufferer, the wanderer was only Conte Giacomo Leopardi, but the poet was Orpheus himself. Long passages are fit to repeat in lieu of prayers through all the watches of the night. How shall I express their quality? Suppose you were held up in some minor Italian town where by chance an itinerant company was to perform *Il Trovatore.* Suppose that having nothing better to do you strolled into the theatre, resigned in advance to a meagre stage-setting, a harsh orchestra, a prima donna past her prime, a rhetorical little tenor saving his breath for the gymnastic prodigy of his final high note. But suppose also that, having found things in general much as you expected, suddenly you heard, coming from behind the wings, an unexampled heavenly voice, a voice pure as moonlight, rich as sorrow, firm as truth, singing 'Solo in terra'. Alone on earth that voice might indeed seem, and far from earth it would carry you; and no matter how commonplace the singer might look, or even ridiculous, when he stepped before the footlights, if ever that sheer music sounded again, there would be something not himself that sang and something not yourself that listened.[65]

In certain states all the random energies of the labouring psyche are magnetised and absorbed into a contemplative stasis, thus perfectly realising the function of spirit. Santayana at one point made the analogy with Aristotle's doctrine of second entelechy,[66] by which Aristotle meant that the act or energy truly characteristic of a rational being has its perfection within itself and does not depend on external movements. There was, however, no undue preponderance of intellectualism in Santayana. Had he not singled out as spiritual beings "poets, mystics or epicureans"?[67] When we consider his doctrine of Essence and Spirit, aesthetic experience may well seem the most helpful tacit model to bear in mind. In such experience psychic energies crystallise into pure attentiveness. Before and after, inner and outer, lose their urgency. The clamorous contingencies of the individual existent fall silent. Persons become states.

The lack of any existential awareness of the individual person in Santayana—unexpected in the writings of a philosopher possessing such a marked personal tone—struck me particularly from the curious way in which he writes of "spirit," as if it were an abstract independent medium absorbing the single fleshly creature into some all-pervading and more rarefied sphere. Perhaps it is to the mystical metaphysics of a Plotinus, whose writings Santayana knew well, that we should turn when trying to grasp this, when Plotinus writes of individual spirits being "inbound with the entire of reality, members of the Intellectual, not fenced off, not cut away, integral to that All."[68] The difficulty is that Santayana's materialist dogmatism forbade his positing any existing One Spirit in which each single spiritual self might participate at the apex of its being. For him, the spiritual factor of consciousness was merely an inexplicable iridescence on a constantly shifting material flux. It was an epiphenomenon. Santayana did not have a great deal that was logically cogent to offer on the body-mind issue, always a thorny one, and in recent years a great favourite with the professionals. But he did have his metaphor of "Realms." Fully focussed mental attention rises toward the Realm of Spirit; its local status is in the Realm of Matter. The mechanism of interaction remains obscure, though plentifully adorned with elevated imagery that prevents him from appearing to be a crude materialist. That imagery, and the contradictions into which it appears to lead him, has the possibly salutary effect of leaving the reader poised over a mystery that no amount of analysis is ever likely to dissolve. On a strict view, however, and especially at a safe distance from the sumptuous fluency of Santayana's style, his terminology suggests flirtation with a substantial spiritual transcendence his materialist outlook does not warrant.

Perhaps it is best to nudge Santayana's reflections in the direction of Phenomenology, which helpfully brackets such ontological dilemmas and asks us simply to attend to qualities of awareness. At a certain point of psychic integration and intensity, one leaves below the distracted ego—an animal automaton pulled this way and that amid a mêlée of spatio-temporal relations, hounded by demons of fear, surmise, and precipitation—and passes into a state of depersonalised awareness: *Reines Wesenschau*. Santayana paid tribute to Husserl in a section of *Realms of Being* and noted the similarities between his own independently excogitated "essences" and the pure "Ideas" of the German founder of Phenomenology, though Santayana drew back from what he saw to be the basically idealist orientation of Husserl. Santayana defined their point of contact by reminding us that for Husserl

objects, in order to enter the realm of this phenomenology, must be thoroughly *purified*. This purification consists in reducing the object to its intrinsic and evident character, disregarding all question of its existence or non-existence, or of its locus in nature; or, in my language, it consists in suspending animal faith, and living instead contemplatively, in the full intuition of some essence. . . . Nothing is therefore removed from experience by purifying it, except its distraction; and an essence, far from being an abstraction from a thing, is the whole of that thing as it ever can be directly given, or spiritually possessed.[69]

The purged immediacy of any spiritual intuition of essence, the "directly given, or spiritually possessed," as Santayana put it, is interestingly brought out in one of the all too few extended passages of concrete example that he gives in *Realms of Being,* where for the most part he moves between abstraction, which is sometimes wearisome, and rhetoric, which is frequently moving and effective in its imaginative fervour but a little unsatisfying from lack of extended illustration. The following passage, however, is helpfully concrete:

Suppose that in a Spanish town I come upon an apparently blind old beggar sitting against a wall, thrumming his feeble guitar, and uttering an occasional hoarse wail by way of singing. It is a sight which I have passed a hundred times unnoticed; but now suddenly I am arrested and seized with a voluminous unreasoning sentiment—call it pity, for want of a better name. An analytic psychologist (I myself, perhaps, in that capacity) might regard my absurd feeling as a compound of the sordid aspect of this beggar and of some obscure bodily sensation in myself, due to lassitude or bile, to a disturbing letter received in the morning, or to the general habit of expecting too little and remembering too much; or if the psychologist was a Freudian, he might invoke some suppressed impression received at the most important period of life, before the age of two. But since that supposed impression is forgotten and those alleged causes are hypothetical, they are no part of what I feel now. What I feel is simply, as Othello says, "the pity of it". And if I stop to decipher what this *it* contains, I may no doubt be led, beyond my first feeling, to various images and romantic perspectives. My fancy might soon be ranging over my whole universe of discourse, over antiquity, over recent wars, over so many things ending in smoke; and my discursive imagery would terminate in dreary cold facts, the prose of history, from which my emotion would have wholly faded. The pity is not for them: it is not for the old man, perhaps a fraud and a dirty miser; it is pity simply, the pity of existence, suffusing, arresting, rendering visionary the spectacle of the moment and spreading blindly outwards, like a light in the dark, towards objects which it does not avail to render distinguishable. There is, then, in this emotion, no composition. There is pregnancy, a quality of having affinity with certain ulterior things rather than with others; but these things are not given; they are not needed in the emotion, which arises absolutely in its full quality and in its strong simplicity. My life might have begun and ended there. Nothing is too complex to be primitive; nothing is too simple to stand alone.[70]

There may be ulterior factors, attendant reflections, and back-ground causes; but all complexities are resolved and transcended by the engulfing synthesis of a spirit purely absorbed in sin-gleness of intuition. "My life might have begun and ended there." That passage contains just a suggestion of a Rilke poem in the making: some condition of pure inwardness distilled from the heartless externality of things. Rilke's heart, however, was always palpitating beneath the exquisitely cut garment of his form, whereas even Santayana's most deeply pondered moments had a touch of chill, something external and aloof in their car-ven eloquence betokening the distance of the surveying con-sciousness from the spectacle it encountered. Had he not written elsewhere that "to pure intuition the living are as ghostly as the dead and the dead as present as the living"?[71] At this point we should take note of his preferred phrasing and imagery in the concluding chapters of *Realms of Being* for conveying the nature of spiritual consciousness.

Daniel Cory once read a statement to Santayana from an article by Paul Claudel in T. S. Eliot's *Criterion:* "Il y a quelque chose en moi qui soit plus moi-même que moi." Claudel's conclusion was that the "quelque chose" was God. When Santayana asked Cory what he thought it might be, Cory re-sponded, half-jokingly, "sex." Santayana, says Cory, smiled pa-tiently at both answers and quietly offered his characteristic term, "spirit."[72] This spirit, the inner self that is superior to the phenomenal ego, or psyche, always figured for Santayana not as agent but as witness: a witness from on high.

The least disciplined or integrated of us sometimes feel something within rising above ourselves, a culmination, a release, a transport beyond distraction. It was but summer lightning, and the sultriness continues unabated; yet that flash has given us a taste of liberty.[73]

The myths about a paradise, past or future, are transparent fables, expressing the rare, transporting, ecstatic quality that distinguishes the

culminating moments of natural life from its endless difficulties, hard-
ships, and embroiled hopes . . . the supreme moment liberates us
from circumstances altogether, and we feel withdrawn into an inner
citadel of insight and exaltation.[74]

[Spirit's] vocation is precisely dominion, spiritual dominion, without distraction, responsibility or power.[75]

If the psyche grows integrated and rational, its centre, which is the
organ of spirit, becomes dominant, and all those eloquent passions
begin to be compared and judged, and their probable issue to be
foreknown and discounted. The waves will not be stilled, but they will
now beat against a rock.[76]

Implicit in all our acts of awareness is an act aware of those
acts. At one point in *The Realm of Spirit,* Santayana makes a
gesture in the direction of Kant's transcendental unity of apper-
ception, a purely logical doctrine, as being analogous to what he
means,[77] but we would probably do better to remember the
Hindu doctrine of the Atman, eternal witness of all the subordinate acts of an ego in partial bondage to Maya: "He is indeed
the pure, the stable, the unmoved, the unaffected, unflurried,
free from desire, standing still like a spectator, self-subsistent"
(Maitri-Upanishad). Our lives are like a stage-play—Santayana
revives the venerable saw for his own ends—and our shifting
moods and opinions so many disguises put on at the behest of a
power not ourselves: "There was something in us always, since
consciousness awoke, that saw our persons as part of the world.
From the beginning there was a moral ambiguity in our souls."
It calls us to see "our passions as follies, our views as illusions,
and identify ourselves not with ourselves, but with the spirit
within us."[78] "In the most masterly mind, in the most victorious soldier or legislator, no profit or peace will come to the
spirit except in pure intuition, when that dominated world and
that brilliant career appear as if in another man's life: a tale, a
vision, in which all passion has become light, and all compulsion deliverance."[79]
Any pure concentrated activity that focusses attention on an
awareness of quality and form, whether it be absorption in a
musical sequence, a mathematical problem, "a breath of morning air or the sum total of possible knowledge,"[80] affords re-

lease from our distracted being as living organisms in the flux of matter, with only the centrifugal surmises of animal faith to guide us. In such concentrated acts of awareness, of sheer attending, we may be said to fulfil perfectly our destiny, which is to be a living flame of pure consciousness.

Santayana's materialist dogmatism precluded any substantial separation of mind from matter, or any teleology in the universe endorsing the supreme reality of mind. Nevertheless, "although each intuition has a date and a home in the physical world, if viewed from the outside or historically, when viewed from within each always stands in the middle of the temporal and spatial universe, introducing a moral centre into a flux where probably no centre exists physically."[81] These consummate acts of conscious existence, though they perfect the function of the individual psyche, and bring it an inner light and happiness, entail as well a certain interior distancing of ourselves from all else that is. Santayana had no time for mystical emotions of fusion with the All; hence his dislike of aspects of Romanticism.[82] To dwell on essence is to dwell on form, something supremely intelligible and discriminated, and such pure distillations of consciousness set us at a remove from the habitual network of external relations in space and time. They show the integration into a single focus of all the purest energies of an individual psyche; they turn all its fuel to light, to use an image of which Santayana was fond. They do not unite us with any other existent being, let alone with the universe, since, as Santayana told Cory in a letter of 1939, when he was near to completing *The Realm of Spirit,*

spiritual union cannot be union with another spirit, but union between spirit in one instance, at one moment, and all things as felt from that point. . . . utter and perfect union has to be momentary and internal to the life of a single soul. It is then not properly union but unification. One really becomes one.[83]

That extremely important and illuminating avowal, made to Cory in a letter, is given extended treatment in the culminating chapter of *Realms of Being* entitled "Union":

That no spirit can absorb any other is evident, since spirit (as I use the word) is an act, not a transferable or transformable substance.

Therefore any spiritual union actually experienced is necessarily specious and a pure datum of intuition. Not that a real union between spirits may not exist, in that separate minds may be unanimous; but this unanimity would be a fact external to their experience of it, a truth about them, which they might conceive and credit, but which could not in itself be a condition or ecstasy attained by either of them. Yet the union that mystics speak of seems to be emphatically a state into which they pass, internal, certain, and overwhelmingly actual. It has the surprising and all-solving character of a datum: and the character of a datum, by definition, is exactly the same whether it happens to be true or merely imaginary. Therefore the only spiritual union that can be certain, obvious, and intrinsically blissful, must be not a union between two spirits but the unity of a spirit within itself.[84]

The last sentence is powerfully suggestive of why Santayana prefaced *Realms of Being* with a technical tour de force of reductive analysis ending in a "solipsism of the present moment."[85] His mind had all along been seeking the utter self-containedness and certainty of such a moment, but on the grandest possible scale. All becomes tributary to the concentrated singleness of a consciousness that dwells with essences "in the eternal." At such a point we feel the curious analogy between Santayana's doctrine of spirit and Hegel's doctrine of Absolute Mind, which subsumes all life and knowledge within a synthesising spiritual whole, in spite of Santayana's irrationalist materialism making him the polar opposite of Hegel in other respects. They meet in a sphere of Gnostic spirituality where consciousness is dominative and liberating.[86] By sublimating all things and persons into essences, Santayana contrived to exist with exalted impartiality in detached contemplation of the varied imaginative goods that the world offers, distilling their qualities in the crucible of his own spirit, integrated and folded in upon itself like that of Marvell's mystical epicurean solitary: "Two paradises 'twere in one / To live in paradise alone." As Edmund Wilson said of the aged Santayana when he met him in Rome in 1946:

His present so triumphant functioning appears to absorb and enchant him. . . .

. . . It would not be precisely true to say that Santayana is narcissistic, but he is interested in his own thought as a personal self-contained system, and in his life as a work of art which owes its integrity and harmony partly to a rigorous avoidance of indiscriminate human relationships.[87]

This may sound like a very "selfish" view of things, but Santayana was at pains to point out—admittedly in a passage that does not quite square with his phrasing elsewhere about the dominative factor in spiritual consciousness—that "spirit by definition is absorbed by the not-self, picturing it, fearing or loving it, living absorbed in its life and form, so that to talk of selfishness in the spirit, in this ideal sense, would be a contradiction in terms."[88] Contemplative discrimination of the qualities of what exists involves a type of imaginative sympathy that enables one to divine the spark of good to which each living thing aspires in its own terms, however bound up it may be with illusion and aggression. (It is perhaps in this light that we should think of Santayana's remark about Communism and Fascism to the *Life* magazine journalist—"doubtless there are good things in both.") In such an Olympian perspective all warring sects become equally justified and equally groundless in their opposition and are "folded in a single party."[89] This disillusioned sympathy with all things for the sake of the goods they seek and may fleetingly embody is what Santayana called "charity," and

charity is a second birth of love, aware of many wills and many troubles. It is not creative or constructive of anything positive, unless it be hospitals and almshouses. Institutions produce rival ambitions, rights, and contentions. About all plans and projects charity is disenchanted and sure only of the ever-present propriety of charity itself.[90]

Santayana praised Dickens by remarking that his most grotesque creatures are not "exaggerations or mockeries of something other than themselves; they arise because nature generates them, like toadstools; they exist because they can't help it, like we all do." The sympathy with which Dickensian humour invests them is for Santayana the sign of a profoundly charitable and spiritual insight. It is a marvellous essay, even though Santayana's incorporation of Dickens into his own chillier substance is not entirely convincing. Santayana's gift was more for harmonising all things within the sovereign sphere of a compassionate cynicism: Machiavelli glinting at us from behind the mask of St. Francis.

Prayer also figures in this lay theology, which contains so much that is sympathetically attuned to the spirit of Catholicism, in spite of an occasional bland reminder that the one is a dogma and his own merely "a language to render articulate the dumb experience of the soul."[91] In prayer we are not so much making petitions, though we may be doing that, too, as "recollecting, digesting and purifying our conscience." In the midst of turbulence spirit disposes us to accept that things may turn out other than we wish, since we depend on a power that some call "God," and that Santayana calls "Matter"; but, in that prayerful resignation to a higher will, "what has happened, what is happening and what is bound to happen fall into a dramatic vista, which the prophet and psalmist deploys eloquently in the prayers; and he judges nothing and promises nothing except as the agent and messenger of God."[92]

Things "fall into a dramatic vista" for the spiritual consciousness, just as all ages form for it "a single panorama."[93] Santayana reverts frequently to the image of a dramatic spectacle or an artistic product to express his sense of the detached godlike spirit in its relation to existence. Of itself the élan vital of existence is senseless, in that no objective good proposed by the intellect, be it social cohesion or the progress of humanity, obliges the constantly shifting forces of living matter to adhere to those goods. Bergson conceded as much in his *Deux Sources de la Moralité et de la Réligion,* and in the margin of his copy of Bergson's book Santayana pencilled a typically ironic comment of agreement: " 'Keep moving' is what this policeman commands. He is not so meddlesome as to tell us which way to move: his orders are 'keep moving', and he sticks to that."[94] In a letter to Bruno Lind, Santayana observed that

Life is essentially an élan vital, as Bergson calls it; that is, it is a *passage* from one state to another. But art, or the immortalisation of life, is a synthesis. You preserve and recompose each episode in the light of the others that accompany or replace it. You make a mosaic or rose-window of history; existence does not carry you on, but becomes truth for you.[95]

Art is a form of charity, too, since in raising phenomenal existence to a significant image of itself, it rescues life from distrac-

tion and endows it with spiritual fulfilment as sheer form, such
as its mixed and broken condition in the transient realm of
matter could never attain.

One may well find oneself asking at this point whether there
is much more in Santayana's final view of things than an eloquent variation on Schopenhauer, whose doctrine of the suspen-
sion of the Will through art and through Buddhistic compassion
must frequently come to mind as one reads the closing chapters
of Santayana's *Realms of Being*. The similarities are undeniable,
and unlikely to have been denied by Santayana, but it is more
just to the latter's individuality to bear in mind the radical
scepticism upon which his contemplative vistas were raised.
Schopenhauer, after all, was a true metaphysician, who held that
he had found a mode of access to the ultimate nature of reality:
through successive affections and acts of our will we gain "in
great measure" knowledge of that thing-in-itself which is the
noumenal Will,[96] whose being, thus intuited, can paradoxically
suspend itself through art and compassion. Schopenhauer
dilated and transmogrified an interior and invisible human faculty, the will, into a cosmic principle of explanation: "Our inner
nature is the will whose *visibility* is matter. . . . Matter is the
visibility of the Will."[97] In however tortuous a fashion,
Schopenhauer was on the high German road of Absolute Idealism to a knowledge of the thing-in-itself.

Santayana's standpoint was different. He was firmly of the
opinion that we have no immediate knowledge of anything
except essences: our discourse *is* our world, one might put it, if
trying to update the point of view. Essences fall into symbolic
systems relative to the organisms in which they chance to arise,
but this brings no knowledge of things-in-themselves. We have
only animal faith, which on one level might be described as the
mere commonsense postulate that an outer world exists and can
be known pragmatically through its responsiveness to our
manipulations of it. But that is not Santayana's usual approach in
the most compelling sections of his later work. He was more
authentically himself when evoking the quality of the world's
presence for the solitary consciousness by means of metaphors
indicating a moral and emotional response: shock, flight, attack,
devouring, restlessness, and so on. Those powerfully evocative

descriptions of the oppressive appearances of Matter were one man's subjectively coloured version of his sense of existence as a predicament and a trap; the fact that the moral colouring of these responses harmonised with certain hallowed traditions of spiritual wisdom gave them no privileged status. They were, at best, evidence of what Ortega y Gasset called "metaphysical sentiment": the essential, ultimate, and basic impression we have of the universe. There was no "truth" in them. Had not Santayana admitted as much in passages from *The Realm of Truth,* when he answered a hypothetical enquiry concerning the truth of his own philosophical system: "No, I reply it is not true, nor meant to be true. It is a grammatical or possibly a poetical construction having, like mathematics or theology, a certain internal vitality and interest"?[98]

No irrationalism[99] could appear more extreme than Santayana's. No scepticism could be more radical. The implications of his formally held views lead one to expect a body of writing that is histrionically fragmented or minutely introverted. In fact, however, from those most unpromising assumptions he elaborated a system of concepts and images overwhelming in its coherence and harmonious eloquence. He seems replete with the disillusioned wisdom of all the great civilisations. So lacquered is the surface that one almost longs at moments for something swift, improvisatory, uncalculated; but that would be fatal to the majestic form asserting itself against the void. His gaze is steady and a mite scornful, his pace deliberate, his every other sentence an epitaph on human hope; yet with an elegantly accommodating gesture he offers us the solace and shelter of a style that blends so smoothly the insights of great mystics, theologians, and metaphysicians that we may end by taking the style for the substance. And perhaps we are right to do so. The style is the man, and we are forced back on our intuitive response to a personality possessed of one steady, intense vision of the tragic predicament of spirit in the world.

Well aware that professionals sneered at his hypnotic style and purple passages, Santayana nevertheless claimed to Cory that the latter were "not applied ornaments but natural growths and *realisations* of the thought previously moving in a limbo of verbal abstractions." "They are," he continued, "imaginative intuitions and they hang together, not by external adjustment, but because they are defined by analysis of an imaginative total, a single unsophisticated vision of the world."[100] "Unsophisticated" gives one a start, admittedly, but the epithet was consistent with another passage in which Santayana out-stared hostile criticism by a yet more primitive avowal. In his autobiography he had said that his philosophy was by no means an artificial academic hypothesis but a set of presuppositions "already alive and at work within me, willy-nilly, like existence itself, and virtually present not only in the boy but in the embryo."[101] Such recourse to the subliminal did not invite argument. Santayana asks us to see his philosophy not as arguing for a set of true propositions but as making a testimony, an assertion. The gap between the spiritual fervour of the assertion and its sceptical and relativistic basis makes for the peculiar tension of an *oeuvre* that otherwise might seem too smoothly rounded. He says gorgeously elevating things in a potentially nihilistic context. I am reminded of a certain kind of Baroque church, on whose facade sunlight carves such grand and generous shapes, behind which lies something sombre and desolate. Yet why not enjoy the facade for what it is? Santayana has a comment on the Baroque style in a volume of his auto-biography, and it has an oblique bearing on the spirit in which we should take his philosophical system:

Bob was a professional architect, with French training: he was dazzled by the picturesque and somewhat religiously moved by the primitives; that was his Anglo-Saxon side; but he was shocked by the false facades of the baroque churches; they were stage settings, allowed to exhibit their shabby side. Yet in persons, as I would tell him, he appreciated the charm and dignity of clothes, which were all *facades* and *postiches*. Why shouldn't buildings, with their meagre material frame-work, expand also into decorative cloaks, ruffs, and *panaches*? There was a kind of homage to the eye and to the ideal in such a seemly masquerade. It presented what it would fain be, and what it thought worthy of your attention. To seem less grand would have been less courteous.[102]

Collingwood remarked in his review of *The Realm of Essence*, when contrasting Santayana's philosophy with Hegel's, that the former's was not so much a system of categories as the elabora-tion of a single point of view described and re-described and described again, never altered or approached or receded from, but held like a great glittering jewel in the writer's hand and scrutinised under every kind of light, turned this way and that and studied in all its aspects as Monet studied his haystack under every hour's varying illumination.[103]

Collingwood went on to say that this is to view a philosophical system as a poem, which he did not think to be a good thing: "Each man's poem may be a genuine intuition of some essence, but poems are not in competition with one another for truth." Collingwood, for all his historicist views, still wrote as a traditional metaphysician for whom philosophers are in search of Truth. Santayana, somewhat paradoxically in view of his spacious rhetoric and old-world graces of manner, was in many respects a more ambiguous and unsettling figure, and thereby congenial, one would think, to the mood of the late twentieth century. Other sceptics and irrationalists leave us naked to the elements, but Santayana constructs for us a habitable illusion, an extensive and elaborate intellectual edifice that the poetic thinker constructs around his own solitude, and that we may share if we feel so inclined. He would not have taken Collingwood's remark amiss.

In his copy of Valéry's *Lettres à Quelqu'un,* now in the rare books collection of Columbia University, Santayana during the last year of his life put strong double-stressed lines of approbation in the margin of two passages. One read: "Pure thought and the search for truth in itself can only ever aspire to the discovery or the construction of a *form.*" In another Valéry expressed irritation, endorsed by Santayana, at the philosopher "who will not avow that all he does is to make a work of art, and who refuses to centre that work *on himself, as he is in fact.* To pretend to be doing anything else is absurd." Valéry added that he preferred this artistic endeavour to be openly avowed as such. Santayana was only too pleased to claim that he had gradually managed "to infuse more and more of myself into the apprehension of the world and its opinions, until in 'Realms of Being' the picture of them becomes itself a confession and an image of the mind that composed it." And he had told Cory that "what I have yearned for all my life is not so much cosmic unity—like Whitehead, but simply 'completion'. If I see a circle half-drawn,

I yearn to complete it"; thereby avowing that harmonious form had been a vital element in his philosophical endeavours.[104] But not the only element. Otherwise he would not count as a philosopher at all.

Aristotle wrote, "If God is always as we are in our good moments, it's a marvellous thing, and if he is more so, it is still more marvellous; but such is the fact." Santayana often gave the impression of being more so: "The one invulnerable man among / Crude captains." Like the Greeks and the Indians, he sought, and on his own terms found, not the peace that passeth all understanding, but the peace that comes through understanding. He settled in his own peculiar fashion for gnosis, not faith. A passage in his autobiography neatly blends the Indian and the Hellenistic affinities present in his outlook. To these we shall turn in the following chapter so as to unravel a little more fully the different strands, both Eastern and Western, that are knit together in an *oeuvre* whose eclectic elements still manage to compose a single rounded emblem of spiritual domination. Santayana tells us how he was offered a choice of mementoes from the library of a recently dead friend, the Harvard poet Trumbull Stickney:

> I asked for his copy—which he had once lent me—of Gade's *Die Sāmkyaphilosophie* [sic]. The gist of these Indian studies was given also in one of Stickney's most interesting poems. A Hindu finds himself in ancient Athens, bewildered by the noise of trade, politics and war, elbowed aside by the rude youths, forsaken and starving. At last in a quiet lane he knocks at a modest door. It is opened by a venerable old man. The stranger is introduced into a walled garden, his bowl is filled with pure rice, and he is left alone to meditate by the trickling fountain. The old man was Epicurus.[105]

· 4 ·

Orientations

IN an essay of the 1940s, "The Idler and His Works," Santayana tells us that "the farther east I looked, the more I discovered my own profound and primitive convictions." We have already learned from his autobiography, written at the same period, that as early as the 1890s he was interested in Garbe's *Die Sāmkhyaphilosophie.* Clearly he had been looking East for a long time. What particularly attracted him to the Sāmkhya among the six classical Hindu schools?

He had written in *Realms of Being* that "at the threshold of natural philosophy the Vedanta must yield to the Sāmkhya."[1] There lies the clue. Sāmkhya was a proto-scientific doctrine, closer in certain respects to the type of Western materialism that Santayana espoused than any other Hindu school. The Sāmkhya granted an independent substantial reality to matter, whose elements it analysed into twenty-four categories. A single term, *antah-karana,* is used to convey the convergence of elements in an empirical ego. This would seem approximately comparable to what Santayana called the "psyche." Like the psyche, *antah-karana* is a dependent manifestation of the primordial homogeneous substance that the Sāmkhya system called *prakrti* and that Santayana called the Realm of Matter. With Sāmkhya there was no suggestion, as with Vedanta, that *prakrti* was a phenomenal mode of one encompassing spiritual reality, Brahman, and that an individual spirit, Atman, was identical in its essence with that ultimate spiritual reality, Brahman. Mystical fusion was alien to the Sāmkhya, as it was to Santayana. Consequently, when we read the following epigraph from one of the Upanishads that Santayana placed at the beginning of his *Realm of Spirit,* we must mentally transpose it into a Sāmkhya context (what Vedanta and Sāmkhya share is the assumption of an impassive consciousness superior to all transient psychic states):

> He who knows Brahma advances towards Brahma everywhere. He comes to the lake of enemies: he crosses it by his mind. When they that know only the present come to the lake, they are drowned. . . . As one driving swiftly in a chariot looks down on the two wheels revolving, so he too looks down on day and night, on good deeds and evil deeds and on all the pairs of contraries. Free from good deeds, free from evil deeds, knowing Brahma, he advances towards Brahma. [*Kaushitaki—Brahmana—Upanishad, 1, 4.*]

Self-transcendence in Sāmkhya was posited for the sake of perfecting the single spirit in isolation, not for the sake of some higher unity in which all separation is overcome, as was the case with Vedanta. Set over against the twenty-four material categories of *prakrti,* a plurality of spiritual monads existed for Sāmkhya, and this realm of spirits, as Santayana might have called it, was known as *purusha,* defined as "a witness; possessed of isolation or freedom; indifferent; a spectator or one who sees; and inactive."[2] *Purusha,* for any self capable of consciousness in the fullest sense, is an eternal spiritual witness of matter and is detached from every subordinate physical and psychic mode of being. This spiritual factor, or *purusha,* in its impartial passivity, implicitly and continuously cancels any identification with the thoughts, affections, and impulses that are the expression of material substance, or *prakrti. Purusha,* in its perfected functioning, withdraws us into a constant, exalted self-annihilation. "Morally, the whole natural world, with our persons in it," Santayana wrote, "will be removed to a distance. It will have become foreign. It will touch us, and exist morally for us, only as the scene of our strange exile, and as being the darkness, the cravings, the confusion in which the spirit finds itself plunged, and from which, with infinite difficulty and uncertainty, it hopes to be delivered."[3]

That passage from Santayana's *Realm of Spirit,* though so close in mood to Sāmkhya and to all Indian doctrines of release from suffering—it comes from a chapter entitled "Liberation"—suggests by the word "morally" a less than total identification with the metaphysical certainties of Indian doctrine. We know from other passages that Santayana resisted the extreme mystical implications of such doctrine, as when in some rough notes on Indian philosophy he remarked that withdrawal from the body into a totally separate realm of spirit was impossible "because none such truly exists." Santayana's materialism was more thoroughgoing than that of the Sāmkhya, since for him spirit was a fluctuating epiphenomenon of matter, not a distinct ontological reality. He also resisted the notion that the perfection of spirit was to dwell with consummate vacuity on nothingness. Spiritual freedom, he said, "consisted in thinking about the congenial and the beautiful, not in not thinking at all." Withdrawal of spirit as advocated by the Sāmkhya was right morally and in principle, but it must be "based on the health of the body (since spirit cannot be severed from it materially) and must terminate in the free life of art and imagination."[4] Such phrasing suggests a humanistic aestheticism supervening on the life of contemplative withdrawal.

That was not the only occasion when Santayana appeared to draw back from the full implications of Indian mystical doctrine, to which the mood of so much of his later writing seems attuned. In an important passage of *The Realm of Essence* he spoke—admittedly not without some self-contradiction and ambiguity—of his own philosophy as "cleaving to the Greeks"[5] rather than following the path of detached contemplation to Pure Being. Such disclaimers are understandable in one who never ceased to see the perfection of existence in the realisation of specific natures rather than their obliteration in a featureless nirvana. His attraction to Sāmkhya must have lain primarily in its doctrine of a plurality of separate spiritual monads, each perfecting itself in isolation, even though he had to qualify its mystical vacuity and its ontological dualism:

Modern philosophy has enabled us to dismiss this notion of an underlying substantial spirit. There is something substantial underlying our feeling and thoughts, but it is the psyche, or the organic life of the body, the substance of which, in its turn, is the common matter of the whole universe. Spirit is as far as possible from being a substance: it is at the other end of the scale, the very flower of appearance, actuality, light and evanesence.[6]

By rather glib recourse to "modern philosophy" Santayana ensures that he distances himself from doctrinal commitment to the East. In practical terms, too, he was at pains to disclaim any similarity in way of life between himself and what he called "the withered Indian gymnosophist." One takes the point. Yet when in Santayana's account the psyche suspends its distracted automatism and rests in some congenial essence, it would seem to achieve by virtue of a certain quality of attention the phenomenological equivalent of the Sāmkhya state of *purusha*. Thus elevated, its life is a series of tales enacted, its destiny that of a wandering stranger amid the hosts of normal madness:

> When in the thick of passion the veil suddenly falls, it leaves us bereft of all we thought ours, smitten and consecrated to an unearthly revelation, walking dead among the living, not knowing what we seem to know, not loving what we seem to love, but already translated into an invisible paradise where none of these things are, but one only companion, smiling and silent, who by day and night stands beside us and shakes his head gently, bidding us say Nay, nay, to all our madness.[7]

Do we have, in Santayana's attempt to adapt Indian perceptions to his Western mode of consciousness, something analogous to a lifelong obsession of Robert Musil that he incorporated in the evolving drama of Ulrich, protagonist of *The Man Without Qualities*? Ulrich, who saw his life "as a stage-décor"; for whom "the quality that clothes have is also possessed by convictions, prejudices, theories, hopes, belief in anything, thoughts";[8] and who sought "the real mind of the mind,"[9] that inward spiritual witness that in certain temperaments always sets at a distance the random movements of the psyche as well as the events of the outer world:

> Revolutions began by promising to create a new civilisation; they make a clean sweep of everything the spirit has achieved to date, as though it were enemy property; and they are overtaken by the next revolution before they can surpass the heights previously attained. So what we called epochs of civilisation are nothing but a long series of signs saying No Road, indicating enterprises that have failed. *And the notion of taking up one's position outside this series was far from new to Ulrich.*[10]

Musil, like Santayana, had been drawn to aspects of mysticism,

Eastern as well as Western, in order to situate a personal intuition not easily accommodated within the self-blinding activism of modern Western civilisation. Though neither ever hinted at a knowledge of the other's writings, it is possible to feel that Santayana's *Realm of Spirit,* the most intensely felt of his later works, would make a telling accompaniment to any perusal of *The Man Without Qualities.* With the possible reservation, however, that Santayana's eloquence on these topics has too perfected a surface, is too classically external, for any extended assimilation to the intricate musings of the Austrian novelist.

A more fitting comparison is with Paul Valéry. His writings Santayana did know and admire, and perhaps it is worth mentioning, too, that the marked affinities between Valéry and Musil have been noted. Without pressing any of the resemblances too far, on account of the differing backgrounds of thought and culture, it is still possible to see the outline of an archetype beginning to take shape: all three were ironic, spectatorial temperaments, attracted toward a detached sphere of consciousness, on the vertical axis.

Much of Valéry's work reveals an obsession with what he called the "Moi-Pur," the element of the self that witnesses and cancels out from some interior spiritual distance the perturbations of the troubled "lower" self: what Santayana called the "psyche" and Valéry "Moi-Trouble." All the latter's desires and aversions are the products of circumstance and chance, something equivalent to the irrational energies of Santayana's "Realm of Matter":

I find no unity in my nature. I do not know its "basis". . . . For what is the basis of my nature, what my nature itself? I can simply aver that I know what I love and I know what I hate, *today.* But in this rôle which my nature has adopted and has imposed on me I see merely an effect of chance. To be conscious of oneself—is that not to feel that one could have been quite other than one is? To feel that one and the same body can make itself available for the numerous rôles which circumstances impose; and the same Self be set against an infinite number of possible combinations, among which must figure all those formed by the mechanical kaleidoscope of dreams? Are we not born of a chance encounter, not of two persons, but of two potentialities, each of whom is the biological quotient of an innumerable number of *others?* Thus I

have a tendency, and a considerable facility, for viewing as accidents—
fundamentally alien to me, really,—my tastes, my aversions, my opinions. . . . I have always only set real store by my Pure Self, by which I
mean the most absolute consciousness, which is a steady and single
process of detaching oneself automatically from everything, and in this
everything I include one's personality, its career, its peculiarities, its
varied powers and pleasures.[11]

If we set those passages, in which Valéry was writing to a
sympathetic priest, beside sections of Santayana's *Realms of Being*
such as now follow, we must surely sense a similarity, even
though Santayana's mode of exposition is less intimate than that
of Valéry, and of necessity more aloofly systematic. The shared
factor is that of a consciousness at hazard to the contingencies of
subliminal force and registering the paradox of its own discon-
tinuities and relativities from some inner spiritual zenith:

Matter, as if ashamed at the irrationality of having one form rather
than another, hastens to exchange it, whatever it may be, for some
other form, and this haste is its whole reality; for it can add nothing to
the essences which it successively exemplifies except just this: that they
are enabled to be exemplified in succession, to be picked up and
abandoned. Matter is the invisible wind which, sweeping for no reason
over the field of essences, raises some of them into a cloud of dust: and
that whirlwind we call existence. . . .

. . . One inert essence after another is thereby embodied in things—
essences inwardly irrelevant, and associated even in thought only when
thought has been tamed and canalised by custom. The method of this
transformation may contain repetitions, and to that extent it will be
mechanical; but it will never become anything but a perpetual genesis
of the unwarrantable out of the contingent, mediated by a material
continuity impartial towards those complications. So the common
man feels that he is the source of his actions and words, though they
spring up in him unbidden; and he weaves a sophisticated moral
personage, all excuses, fictions, and verbal motives, to cover the
unknown currents of his material life. Philosophers are not wanting to
do the same for mankind at large, or even for the universe.[12]

Valéry's most famous dramatisation of his sense of the hazardous, irrational contingency of matter, similar to what Santayana conveys in that passage of *Realms of Being*, was *Monsieur
Teste*. Teste was a caricature of one extreme to which Valéry's

resentment of irrational emotion and rhetoric carried him: an austerely mathematical nihilist who can come to terms with the contingent only by treating it as material for frozen calculations of will and power. More satisfying, however, than the attentuated ironies of *Monsieur Teste,* and closer to an important aspect of Santayana, is Valéry's poem, *La Jeune Parque.* Neither Valéry nor Santayana held simplistic Cartesian views of consciousness. Santayana's "Spirit" is the spontaneous self-expression of the realm of material and biological forces that morally can be such a torment and distraction to it; only an organic sensibility can issue in the supremely natural harmony that we call spiritual and contemplative transcendence. A passage from the Preface to *Realms of Being* reminds us that in spite of the Manichean rhetoric he often used to convey the torments of spirit amid material existence, Santayana always envisaged the possibility of harmony in the relationship of those intricately interdepending factors. Thereby he showed himself instinctively attuned to Sāmkhya doctrine, for which *prakṛti* and *purusha* are co-efficient factors rather than contradictory opponents. Their fated and fruitful complicity Santayana conveys thus:

It is so simple to exist, to be what one is for no reason, to engulf all questions and answers in the rush of being that sustains them. Henceforth nature and spirit can play together like mother and child, each marvellously pleasant to the other, yet deeply unintelligible; for as she created him she knew not how, merely by smiling in her dreams, so in awaking and smiling back he somehow understands her; at least he is all the understanding she has of herself.[13]

The note struck has an affinity with the bitter-sweet reconciliation near the ending of Valéry's *La Jeune Parque,* when cold, disdainful consciousness acknowledges its dependence on the threatening riches of the subliminal realm. It is toward a creative interpenetration between the Self and the Other—Spirit and Matter—that Valéry's poem obscurely tends:

> Doucement,
> Me voici: mon front touche à ce consentement. . . .
> Ce corps, je lui pardonne, et je goûte à la cendre.
> Je me remets entière au bonheur de descendre,
> Ouverte aux noirs témoins, les bras suppliciés,

Entre des mots sans fin, sans moi, balbutiés. . . .
Dors, ma sagesse, dors. Forme-toi cette absence;
Retourne dans le germe et la sombre innocence.
Abandonne-toi vive aux serpents, aux trésors. . . .
Dors toujours! Descends, dors toujours! Descends,
  dors, dors![14]

Valéry explores the issues with more disturbing subtlety than Santayana, who was a speculative rhetorician of superb scope and incisiveness rather than a great poet of the intimate psychological depths. Here again we sense a missing dimension in Santayana, as when comparing him with Musil. Yet what he lacked in anguished penetrative profundity he made up for by a serenely comprehensive grasp of all the issues at stake. These were religious issues, arising in the secularised milieu of the Western world in the late nineteenth and the twentieth centuries.

We witness in Santayana, as well as in Valéry and in Musil, all of whose detached sceptical relativism was a product of the European Enlightenment, a revulsion against the secularism which that very Enlightenment had bred. They did not, however, strike conventional attitudes of rejection in the romantic-primitive or romantic-reactionary modes, but registered their alienation from the modern worship of process by strategies of spiritual transcendence that interiorise traditional notions of the divine. The affinities to be sensed in all three with aspects of Oriental speculation as well as Western mystical theology are clear. All were repelled by modern fixation on development along the horizontal plane, whether in the now widely discredited pseudo-scientific version of Marxism or in the more loosely held simplistic faith in secular progress that flourished until the early years of the twentieth century. During his European travels in the 1900s Santayana had come upon a little scene that crystallised for him the vulgar impiety of secular progressivism, and he recounted it in his autobiography:

At Paestum there was only the railway station and no hotel, but travellers might spend the night comfortably at La Cava, not far away. I had done so and in the morning was waiting at the station for the train to Naples. The only other persons on the platform were a short fat middle-aged man and a little girl, evidently his daughter. In the stillness of the country air I could hear their conversation. The child was asking questions about the railway buildings, the rails, and the switches. 'Where does that other line go?' she asked as if the matter interested her greatly. 'Oh, you can see,' the father replied, slightly bored. 'It runs into that warehouse.' 'It doesn't go beyond?' 'No. It stops there.' 'And where does this line go?' 'To Naples.' 'And does it end there?' 'No, it never ends. It goes on forever.' *'Non finisce mai?'* the girl repeated in a changed voice. *'Allora Iddio l'ha fatto?'* 'No,' said her father dryly, 'God didn't make it. It was made by the hand of man. *Le braccia dell'uomo l'hanno fatto.'* And he puffed his cigar with a de-fiant resentful self-satisfaction as if he were addressing a meeting of conspirators.

I could understand the irritation of this vulgarian, disturbed in his secret thoughts by so many childish questions. He was some small official or tradesman of the Left, probably a Freemason, and proud to utter the great truth that man had made the railway. God might have made the stars and the deserts and all other useless things, but every-thing good and progressive was the work of man. And it had been mere impatience that led him to say that the Naples line never ended. Of course it couldn't run on forever in a straight line. The child must have known that the earth is round, and that the continents are sur-rounded by water. The railways must stop at the sea, or come round in a circle. But the poor little girl's imagination had been excited and deranged by religious fables. When would such follies die out?

Commonplaces that had been dinned all my life into my ears: yet somehow this little scene shocked me. I saw the claw of Satan strike that child's soul and try to kill the idea of God in it. Why should I mind that? Was the idea of God alive at all in me? No: if you mean the traditional idea. But that was a symbol, vague, variable, mythical, anthropomorphic; the symbol for an overwhelming reality, a symbol that named and unified in human speech the incalculable powers on which our destiny depends. To observe, record, and measure the method by which these powers operate is not to banish the idea of God; it is what the Hebrews called meditating on his ways. The modern hatred of religion is not, like that of the Greek philosophers, a hatred of poetry, for which they wished to substitute cosmology, mathematics, or dialectic, still maintaining the reverence of man for what is superhuman. The modern hatred of religion is hatred of the truth, hatred of all sublimity, hatred of the laughter of the gods. It is puerile human vanity trying to justify itself by a lie. Here, then, most opportunely at the railway station returning from Paestum, where I had been admiring the courage and the dignity with which the Dorians recognised their place in nature, and filled it to perfection, I found the brutal expression of the opposite mood, the mood of impatience, conceit, low-minded ambition, mechanical inflation, and the worship of material comforts.[15]

Santayana was far from being unappreciative of the material comforts, transformations, and ingenuities that are the triumphant practical expression of the secular spirit in modern Western civilisation. In this he resembled Valéry and Musil. None had any time for the blowsy mysticism and contempt for science that were offshoots of the romantic movement. Because they were in important respects products of the European Enlightenment, their attitude to the scientific naturalism that was one of its main impulses could be only an ambiguous one. In Santayana's case this took the shape of a firm rejection of dogmatic supernaturalism along with an abiding sense of piety before the chthonic and cosmic powers such as we can only call "religious." Yet the irrational source of all contingency, which was the nearest thing Santayana came to worshipping, did not have the attributes of God in a moral sense. There was no suggestion of a loving Father. There was only an unfathomable presence, best endured by being transmuted into the inwardness of spirit. In a semi-mythical passage evocative of neo-Platonism, Santayana wrote:

On this hint we might sketch the earthly round of spirit, descending from heaven empty and open to every illusion, and ascending into heaven full, but thoroughly purified. A deep pre-natal sleep might be first broken by a feeling of pressure, which if intensified would become pain. A sense of inescapable duration, a dread of change or a longing for it, would create temporal perspectives, forward and back, into an oncoming future and a receding past, both ambiguously present, and both unseizable. These would form a ghostly world, to which spirit somehow would feel that it belonged, and from which the real world would be hard to disentangle. Yet those vital emotions and those temporal perspectives would have had no consistence, if they had contained no images, and supplied no recognizable ideal terms in which spirit might describe them. Nature and history would thus gradually take shape before the distracted spirit and would reveal to it the secret of its own destiny. Anxiety and craving would dissolve before this redeeming knowledge, and the universe would be clarified into a complex essence, given pure and untroubled to intuition. Spirit, so enlightened, would be again at peace.[16]

Such a passage could obviously be related to Indian doctrines of subjugation to Maya, but its affinity with similar strains in Occidental speculation in the Hellenistic phase of classical antiquity is just as evident. These have been touched on in passing at several points in earlier chapters, but some further comments may help us relate Santayana more closely to that context.

The notion of spiritual life as a stranger dwelling in a lower world of illusion was not peculiar to the East. Hellenism after the decline of the city-state was permeated by schemes of individual salvation through philosophical withdrawal from the world, and eventually by Gnostic beliefs in redemption from the lower realm of matter through revealed spiritual illumination. Santayana, who confessed to finding late Hellenism a congenial milieu for his imagination, of course knew perfectly well that the writings of Plato and Aristotle, the object of his special admiration, were still grounded in the civic ideals of the city-state. As he put it in *Platonism and the Spiritual Life:* "After having been very poetical Plato became very austere; but his philosophy remained political to the end. To this descendent of Solon the universe could never be anything but a crystal case to hold the jewel of a Greek city."[17] Nevertheless Santayana cannot have been unmindful of a famous passage in Plato's *Republic* that prefigured the attitude of spiritual withdrawal and world-rejection among numerous later sages of the ancient world. Plato compared the sage to

a man who has fallen among wild beasts—he will not join the wickedness of his fellows, but neither is he able singly to resist all their fierce natures, and therefore seeing he would be of no use to the State or to his friends, and reflecting that he would have to throw away his life without doing any good to himself or others, he holds his peace, and goes his own way. He is like one who, in the storm of dust and sleet which the driving wind hurries along, retires under the shelter of a wall; and seeing the rest of mankind full of wickedness, he is content if only he can live a life pure from evil and unrighteousness, and depart in peace and goodwill with bright hopes.[18]

One is naturally reminded when reading those lines, in which existence is compared to a violent and irrational force, of Santayana's similar image of the "whirlwind of existence";[19] and

Plato's wise man who retreats under a wall is close in spirit to the defensive yet dominative images Santayana used to define the spiritual life. Pertinent as well is a remark of Socrates in Plato's *Theaitetos:*

> Evils . . . can never be abolished, for the good must always have its opposite. Nor is there room for them in the divine world, but they must needs haunt this world of our mortality. And it behoves us with all haste to flee the earth for an immortal home, in other words to make ourselves like unto the divine so far as that may be.[20]

Had not Santayana written in an early essay on Plotinus, during the relatively peaceful era prior to the First World War, that "the Platonic good is the goal of a very special aspiration, now largely in abeyance. But things come round in this world; the ruffians may be upon us some day when we least expect it, and philosophy has to retire to the sanctuary again"?[21]

"Things come round in this world." The casual phrase tells us how attuned Santayana's nature was to an ancient view of history as, at best, cyclical: progressing toward a phase of maturity and then declining, more or less violently, into inevitable chaos. It also tells us how little faith he had in any of the historical vistas of Judaeo-Christianity that depicted the world-process as a progressive sifting and winnowing, culminating in a wholly transformed condition for humanity. It need hardly be added that the modern secularised versions of such doctrines of humanity's progress were meaningless to him. Santayana was not anti-Semitic in any deeply damaging sense, but he was scornful of Jewish prophetic hopes of an earthly consummation of righteousness in the future, and indicted the Jews for worshipping prosperity and worldliness. What Santayana denigrated was given a very different interpretation by Eugène Ionesco, whose remarks call into question the whole supratemporal attitude to salvation that Santayana admired in the Indians and in the Hellenistic sages:

> I therefore believe that without the Jews, the world would be harsh and sad. What keeps us alive? The hope that some day or other, everyone will change, and everything will change and be good and beautiful. Without the Jews, we should not have this belief: we should not hope in the coming or the return of a Messiah, the saviour. We still

hope, knowing that the Messiah is behind the door: we hope that he
will open it one day and that the world will be flooded with joy and
light. We all hope in the ideal City, that is to say we all hope that a new
Jerusalem will rise up from the deserts and from death. We hope for the
transfiguration of the world, and we shall hope for this as long as there
are Jews. Without them, madness of crime; without them, darkness.[22]

Ionesco's words find their echo in a remark of Edwyn Bevan in
his book on Hellenistic antiquity. He missed, he said, any sense
among its intelligentsia of hope in a world-transforming cause,
and the effect on him of the mood of withdrawal and superiority to fortune, both Indian and Hellenistic, was that of the
"quietness of death."[23] Santayana, with his marvellously flexible and comprehensive intelligence, was well aware of that
possibility in the life he had chosen, following in the path of
many consecrated minds in the past, both Eastern and Western.
He noted its sad inevitability in these words, at the end of his
life:

I know very well that this philosophic salvation is not such as nature
or life looks for or can accept: it is only what the truth affords to the
spirit. Life and nature do not ask to be saved from themselves: they ask
only to run on at full tilt. It is the spirit that asks to be saved from that
insane predicament. Yet spirit is an emanation of life, and it is more
truly and naturally happy in the first phases of its career than in its final
salvation. In the end, when it has understood and renounced everything, if you ask it whether it is happy, it can reply only as La Vallière
replied to the friends who asked her if she were happy in the Carmelite
convent to which she had retired: *Je ne suis pas heureuse; je suis contente.*[24]

Contentment is a stable thing, a classical attainment, opposed
both to the fervours of messianic hope and to the volatile
ecstasies of romantic vitalism. Santayana inherited from the
Greeks their preference for the enduring and the eternal, which
they placed either in the intellectual apprehension of forms and
universals—part of what Santayana meant by essences—or in
ecstatic union with a single principle grounding all forms:
Plato's Good, Plotinus' One. "True happiness is not vague and
fluid," Plotinus wrote, "it is an unchanging state."[25] Plotinus
had abandoned the quest to realise the good in the city of men.
All practical virtues were propaedeutic to absorption in eternal

things. "To put Happiness in actions is to put it in things that are outside the Soul; for the Soul's expression is not in action but in wisdom, in a contemplative operation within itself; and this, this alone, is Happiness."[26] Thus Plotinus. "The only spiritual union that can be certain, obvious, and intrinsically blissful," Santayana had written, "must be not union between two spirits but the unity of a spirit within itself."[27]

Plotinus was still enough of a Greek contemplative in the classical tradition to retain a reverence for the physical cosmos as a harmonious expression of the eternal, "a beautiful visible god," as Plato put it in the *Timaeus*.[28] Yet Plotinus, even though he wrote a treatise against the Gnostics, by his relegation of all activity other than contemplation of the eternal to inferior stages of the soul's journey from embodiment to pure spirit was drawing close to the fundamental orientation of ancient Gnosticism, with its belief that the material world is a place of darkness and exile.

The notion of spirit as a stranger in the world, a favourite one with Santayana, for whom an epiphenomenal spirituality assumed the role of ontologically transcendent divinity, is all-pervasive in Gnosticism. A modern authority has stressed that one of the permanent characteristics of Gnostic thought is the opposition it makes between creation and God. God has no relation with the world because any such relation would impair His status and sully His purity. The world is not of God's doing, nor is it the object of His providential concern.

If he intervenes in the world it is in order to offer salvation from the world, to arrange an escape from the world, not to accomplish anything at all through the world. This transcendent God—compared by the Christian polemicists to the *Deus Otiosus* of Epicurus—is thus a stranger to the world and its history: he is, in the very terms of the Gnostics, the Stranger God.[29]

Ancient Gnosticism, whether pagan or heretically Christian, was frankly magical in its depiction of the spirit's imprisonment in a lower world of matter ruled by demonic powers. In its flourishing mythological accretions of aeons and demons and angels between that lower world and the transcendent brightness of an invisible God of pure light, it was far removed from the firmly naturalistic outlook of Santayana. The phantastic cosmological speculations of Hinduism were alien to him as well, and he specifically detached himself from any such superstitious extravagance.[30] Steady retention of a naturalistic base reminds us that Santayana managed in his later writings to sustain by poetical phasing, and at times by virtual self-contradiction, an intensely felt paradox: redemptive spirituality within the framework of an intransigently monistic materialism. All real causal efficacy lies in the realm of matter, and spirit is an epiphenomenon of matter at the mercy of external relations; yet spirit at certain phases and in certain temperaments may reach a harmonious integration of powers that detaches it from the distractions of animal faith so as to attain a virtual interior transcendence of its material nexus. A stranger, it lives as if pure spirit, even though it is not substantially so. Such spiritual life need not dwell only on the heights, like the mystic absorbed in his vision of Pure Being. It may come to a musician absorbed in his art, or to a child at play. It is activity free, pure, and self-justifying. It is both fruition and release. A passage at the beginning of *Realms of Being* crystallises Santayana's meaning in an image:

The stimulus that calls animal attention to some external fact, in provoking an act of the body, also presents some image to the mind. Moreover this labour of perception may be more or less welcome, pleasant, or life-enhancing, apart from its ulterior uses; and sometimes this incidental emotion is so strong that it overpowers the interest which I may have had originally in the external facts; and, I may suspend my action or continue it automatically, while my thought is absorbed in the image and arrested there. As I was jogging to market in my village cart, beauty has burst upon me and the reins have dropped from my hands. I am transported, in a certain measure, into a state of trance. I see with extraordinary clearness, yet what I see seems strange and wonderful, because I no longer look in order to understand, but only in order to see. I have lost my preoccupation with fact, and am contemplating an essence.[31]

The serenity of such a paragraph should not lead us to forget, however, how frequently Santayana conveys the passage from the practical to the spiritual mode of attending with an emotional violence of phrasing that suggests a Gnostic disposition.

As when he writes of spirit's recovering its independence, relating to its transcendental station, and wondering at the "bewitchment that could seem to disperse it so helplessly amid all those beasts and all those catastrophes";[32] of spirit's being "mangled in the hideous mad-house of the world";[33] and, most Gnostic of all: "The true sin is cosmic and constitutional; it is the heritage of Chaos. This is the sin of which spirit is the innocent victim."[34]

From the dark and awesome fatality of existence Santayana kept open a door of retreat to the "inner citadel of insight and exaltation."[35]

A possible liberation ideally, in the vertical direction, when at any moment or habitually, the spirit in a man recalls its universality, its merely momentary lodgment here, or pre-occupation with this trouble, and expands intuitively into the equilibrium of all moments, and the convergence of all insights, under the intense firmament of truth.[36]

All the movements of thought with which it has been tempting to align Santayana's peculiar position—Gnosticism, aspects of Platonism and neo-Platonism, Catholic Christianity insofar as it retained a neo-Platonic colouring, the Indian Sāmkhya—state or imply that elect and illuminated beings can attain a transcendence of cosmic fatality, and gaze down on the spectacle of a lower world that includes not only external things, but also the varied dispositions of their own lower natures, in the spirit of an actor who can view with a certain sublime detachment all the variety of his roles and gestures.

The life-as-stage-play "topos" is very common in the world-views we are considering. It can make for a certain lightness of spirit in response to the contingent roles that existence may chance to assign us. Of all people, the Plato of *The Laws* must not be taken as suggesting that things are really a bit of a giggle, yet even that most austere exemplar of the tradition concerned adjures us to "keep our seriousness for serious things, and not waste it on trifles, and that, while God is the real goal of all serious endeavour, man has been constructed as a toy for God, and this is, in fact, the finest thing about him. All of us, then, men and women alike, must fall in with our rôles."[37]

The transcendence of the contingent to which Plato lays claim is of a type not strictly available to Santayana; hence the tincture of aestheticism we may feel to be endemic to his whole exalted enterprise. Yet in his own elegantly aloof way he gives telling expression in an essay entitled "Carnival" to the ultimate levity that is the only acceptable seriousness about mundane existence:

> Existence is indeed distinguishable from the platonic essences that are embodied in it precisely by being a conjunction of things mutually irrelevant, a chapter of incidents, a medley improvised here and now for no reason, to the exclusion of the myriad other farces which, so far as their ideal structure is concerned, might have been performed just as well. This world is contingency and absurdity incarnate, the oddest of possibilities masquerading momentarily as a fact.[38]

It should not surprise us that lightness of heart, *désinvolture,* and a sense of fun were qualities Santayana valued; they seemed to him truer signs of a spiritual being than any amount of solemn self-importance. It has more than once struck me how tempting it might appear to depict him in a way appealing to twentieth-century intellectual *Angst:* his sense of the irrational absurdity of existence; his radical epistemological scepticism; his Nietzschean moral perspectivism; his sense of discourse as symbolism bearing no satisfying correspondence to a given set of outer facts; the despair of any certainty thereby induced. Yet those seemingly disintegrating factors are neutralised through a poised detachment that is the token of his belonging, even if only aesthetically, to the older tradition of spiritual transcendence that has been our point of reference. There was no agitated anguish. There was the smile of Parmenides, "the ironic smile at the universal joke."[39] His dry, tolerant wit was a part of that mood. So, too, was his liking for the gift of laughter. He liked it in others, and he had it himself. In his autobiography he remembered its presence in a young friend, and in his half-sister, Susana, and then he broadened the implications of the gift:

> There was an important element in Warwick, however, that didn't appear in Bayley: Warwick was full of laughter. Now laughter, as I have come to see in my old age, is the innocent youthful side of repentance, of disillusion, of understanding. It liberates incidentally, as spiritual insight liberates radically and morally. Susana also was full of laughter; it was the deepest bond between us. By laughing together we would

erase the traces of any divergence or failure of sympathy. At the same time, Susana, like Bayley and Warwick, was devout; this marked their sensitiveness to the Good, their capacity to worship. These were the two prerequisites, in my conception, to perfect friendship; capacity to worship and capacity to laugh. They were the two windows through which the mind took flight and morally escaped from this world.[40]

Between the laughing and the weeping philosopher there is no opposition; *the same facts* that make one laugh make one weep. No whole-hearted man, no sane art, can be limited to either mood. In me this combination seems to be readier and more pervasive than in most people. I laugh a great deal, laugh too much, my friends tell me; and those who don't understand me think that this merriment contradicts my disillusioned philosophy. *They,* apparently, would never laugh if they admitted that life is a dream, that men are animated automata, and that the forms of good and beautiful are as various and evanescent as the natural harmonies that produce them. They think they would collapse or turn to stone, or despair and commit suicide. But probably they would do no such thing; they would adapt themselves to the reality, and laugh.[41]

We may feel in the second passage that laughing tolerance borders on contempt for the poor forked human animal, and that Santayana is rather unnervingly like the insouciant epicurean deity of Lucretius: "Privata dolore omni, privata periclis / ipsa suis pollens opibus, nil indiga nostri."★ An impish hardness showed its claws at times. Gore Vidal recorded one example when he went to see Santayana in Rome just at the end of the Second World War:

Even at eighty-five the clear black eyes shone as bright and as hard as obsidian. When I said to him with youthful despair, that the world had never yet been in so terrible a state Santayana could not have been more brisk, or chilling. "My own life-time has been spent in a longer period of peace and security than that of almost anyone I could conceive of in the European past." When I spoke with horror and revulsion of the possibility that Italy . . . Bella Italia . . . might go communist in the next month's election, Santayana looked positively gleeful. "Oh let them! Let them try it! They've tried everything else so why not communism? After all who knows what new loyalties will emerge as

★Without pain, without danger, mighty from his own resources, needing us not at all. [Author's translation.]

they become part of a wolf pack." I was sickened and revolted by his sang-froid, his cynicism.[42]

It is quite something to have shocked Gore Vidal. He should have reminded himself of the ferocious moral relativism that lurked beneath the imperturbable upper spaces of the philosopher's spiritual detachment. Santayana had a decided preference for the particular virtues to which nearly two thousand years of Catholic Christendom had disciplined the human heart; and he hoped for their resurgence in the centuries to come,[43] though without any great faith in this happening. He did not, however, for a moment believe that these virtues had a special privilege in the fertile chaos of matter, since every beautiful accomplishment depends on the irrational, constantly changing momentum of existence:

Precept divides the moral world materially into right and wrong things; but nothing concrete is right or wrong intrinsically, and every object or event has both good and bad effects in the context of nature. Every passion, like life as a whole, has its feet in one moral climate and its head in another. Existence itself is not a good, but only an opportunity. Christians thank God for their creation, preservation, and all the blessings of this life, but life is the condition and source of all evil, and the Indians thank Brahma or Buddha for lifting them out of it. What metaphysical psychologists call Will is the great original sin, the unaccountable and irrational interest which the spirit takes, when it is incarnate, in one thing happening rather than another; yet this mad interest is the condition of generosity and of every virtue. Love is a red devil at one end of its spectrum and an ultra-violet angel at the other end.[44]

The concluding image of dangerous depths and pure intense summit is very characteristic of Santayana. His sympathies in that passage clearly lie with Hinduism and Buddhism, and he dissociates them both from the factor that is distinctive of Christianity: its doctrine of the essential goodness of creation that, though flawed by sin, the Creator saw fit to sanctify and redeem by His fleshly presence. How then in old age did Santayana come to terms with Christianity, and more specifically with the figure of Christ, in his book on the Gospels?

In brief the answer is this: he came to terms with them as the

Gnostics did in the early centuries of the faith. Scholars seem generally to accept that heretical Christian Gnosticism of the second and third centuries A.D. was an attempt to adapt the insights of a pessimistic dualism deriving from syncretistic Greek and Oriental sources to the peculiar facts of the Christian revelation. When speculations about the imprisoned spirit making its escape from the evil darkness of matter toward the higher spheres of light came into contact with the historical facts of Christ's life and His continuing presence in the community of the Church, they tended to transform the incarnate Christ into a purely spiritual principle, or Logos, contact with which sets in motion the Gnostic illumination. They turned away from the dense and fleshly realities of Christian salvation. And Santayana wrote of Christ's nature that "the centre is divine, and what is put on like a garment or a dramatic mask is human nature."[45]

That is very much in the spirit of Gnosticism. What Santayana does throughout his book on the Gospels is turn the nature and sayings of Christ into an allegory of his own philosophy of spirit's incarnation in the world. He says at one point that the transition from Hebrew Messiah to Christian Redeemer was facilitated by the philosophical schemes of salvation already present in the pagan world—

not of course philosophy of the modern kind, but the enacted personal philosophy or enlightened life of the ancients. . . . Christ could never have attracted the faith and love of that dissolving world if he had seemed less heroic than the stoic sage, less detached than the sceptic, or less sensitive than the poetic epicurean.[46]

One sees the features of Christ beginning to assume the kindly scorn of a certain twentieth-century philosopher housed on the Monte Celio in Rome. Louis Bouyer's diagnosis is surely true, and the one most apt for seeing what Santayana is doing: "In the heretical Christian gnosis the element of ancient spirituality which was the least tractable to the Gospel strove to correct the Gospel in order to reduce it by force to a framework that it could not shatter."[47]

For the ancient spirituality to which Bouyer refers, salvation consisted in illuminated knowledge for an elect few who are intrinsically inhabitants of the world of light. Salvation was not from sin, but from fate. Grace given or withheld by a God who created matter as good and who offered Himself to faith in the actual suffering body of a Galilean peasant, during a specific period of thirty-odd years in a particular province of the Roman Empire, was a dimension of Christianity that the Gnostic temperament found hard to accept. The God of historical Christian faith draws all things to Himself as a centre, whereas, as Stephen Neill has written, "it is certain that for Gnosticism in all its forms man is at the centre of the picture; it deals with permanent and unchanging factors in the human situation, and to it history is a matter of supreme indifference."[48] Santayana comments, very much in that spirit:

Jesus had been the true Christ precisely because he did not fulfil literally the promises of the prophets—a fulfilment which would have been only a complication of vanities—but founded a gnostic religion, revealing the secret of that spiritual universe which those prophecies had signified in barbaric symbols.[49]

Naturally Santayana did not blandly set aside the whole historical dimension of New Testament Christianity in order to substitute for it the mythological phantasies of the Gnostics in any literal sense. Nevertheless his sympathy with the essential spirit of the Gnostic treatment of Christ is clear, and for him the mystery of God-in-Man is "a symbol for the high moral and ontological mysteries which it personifies";[50] and he tells us at another point that the kingdom of God will arrive "by an absolute passivity, a perfect purity taking possession of the inner man."[51] Christ seems to begin to approximate certain aspects of *purusha* in the Hindu Sāmkhya, or of Spirit in Santayana's philosophy: impartial witness of the vicissitudes of material fate; incarnate, in that any individual spirit must assume a station in a particular material organism at a given time and place; suffering in the confinement of its incarnate role, but by its godlike element transcending those limitations and living in imagination *sub specie aeternitatis:*

There is therefore one strain in human nature that craves union with God at God's level. It may be called reason, but it does not proceed by reasoning. It may be called love, but it claims possession of nothing. It is that free life of the spirit which continually peeps out in intelligence and in laughter, only to be smothered again in the press of affairs. This is the element in us that we have distinguished and hypostasised in the idea of pure spirit. Spirit in us drinks in and watches all the vicissitudes of fortune, suffering them all; but suffering them, as it were, from above, innocently and without contamination, as Christ endured everything human. For it is in the nature of spirit to transmute the physical impressions made on us by events into images and into enduring knowledge. God became man precisely to undergo and to transcend all that man may have to endure: and in Christ the spirit rises again to God with all its human burden, in order to preserve and eternalise this humanity, as spirit alone can, clearly, victoriously, and in peace.[52]

The ambiguities that surround Santayana's use of the word "God" are apparent in that passage. When spirit arrests and records transient things in images that reveal their eternal being as essences, the spirit may be said to "rise again to God," in that it performs a godlike role. Nevertheless spirit is dependent for its own activities on a factor other than itself, which is godlike in the sense of being impersonally omnificent: what Santayana called Matter. Matter is unconcerned with such spiritual goods as it may chance to generate. Santayana was quite content to use the alternative names God, or Matter, or the External World; each for him was only a symbol for the unknowable depths encountered pragmatically through animal faith. His wording varied, however, in its emotional attitude to that mysterious source of our being. At times he wrote with something of the horror and fear of the Gnostic about the dark irrational fatality that frustrates the attainment of spiritual illumination and peace. At other times something of playfulness and serenity came into his phrasing as he dwelt on the interdependence, the almost affectionate complicity, between spirit and matter. On yet other occasions primitive awe and piety at our dependence on the great irrational Other took possession of his pen; and he seemed then more impressed by the Judaeo-Christian symbolism for ultimate and divine things than by the Greek, because the Socratic element in Greek culture was a nostalgic rationalism and could not truly be reconciled to the irrational generative powers governing existence:

In many of the parables this absolute prerogative of God appears, which places him and his decrees beyond the reach of our wishes or reason or sense of justice. The representation of God as an absolute monarch, or as a loving father, is obviously mythical; yet it brings us more squarely before the facts of moral life than does, for instance, the philosophy of Socrates. Socrates was a rationalist, and abandoned his first master Anaxagoras, when he found that this philosopher spoke of the sun and moon as if they were stones, without disclosing the *reason* why they existed and shone so conveniently upon us. Now reason is an admirable method by which to integrate our minds and characters, and adapt our arts to the potentialities of matter; but reason imposed on the universe is madness, because existence is necessarily irrational. Internally the world may be as methodical and regular and calculable as it likes; yet *that it is so* will remain a perfectly arbitrary fact; and we shall soon come upon elementary data, absolutely groundless, for reason to play upon, if it is not to perish by a flight into thin air. Such flights are not forbidden to the human spirit in dreams, and in certain pure arts without fixed models, like music and poetry. These are the creations of freedom and the arts of leisure. The philosophy of Socrates, and all metaphysical rationalism partake of this luxurious character. In them a high mental civilization overleaps its bounds, and attempts to enclose the universe within human logic and human fancy. Among the Jews the circumstance of not being speculative saved religion and literature from this danger. God was irresponsible power, as nature actually is. He was kindly, but jealous and irascible: he prescribed laws and limits, but remained free to change or enlarge them.[53]

The last words seem to allow for the arbitrariness of Grace, and the unpredictability of God taken as ultimate power. Occasionally, and obscurely, one finds oneself asking whether the irrationalism of Santayana's primary intuition may have been a devious way of acknowledging dependence on a being whose mystery he would not contaminate by confining it within human predication or prediction. His scepticism, and his consequent dependence on animal faith, may then strike us as indications of an obscure yet ardent religious feeling; his moral relativism as a refusal to allow limited human preferences to take possession of the ways of the divine. It might bring to mind the theology of a William of Ockham, for whom God's absolute power pre-empts all reason. Such speculations are probably better not pressed. Better also, perhaps, not to be too carried away by all that is tender and profound in Santayana's response to the Gospels. It shows much sympathetic insight into Christ's love for those who have no false pretence of human dignity and abandon themselves to divine power; for sinners; for the Prodigal Son. Suffice it to say that some of *The Idea of Christ in the Gospels* seems unaffected by the tendentiousness of Santayana's Gnostic thesis. One can well understand why Catholics have never ceased to be concerned for his ultimate religious dispositions. Certainly in him we have to do with no superficial sceptic or humanist, but with a profoundly enigmatic and intense religious temperament.

It was with a specially serious eloquence that he conveyed his intimation of divine power in the memorial address on Spinoza, delivered at the *Domus Spinoziana* in The Hague in 1932:

The spirit has perceived that though it is living, it is powerless to live; that though it may die, it is powerless to die; and that altogether, at every instant and in every particular, it is in the hands of some alien and inscrutable power.

Of this felt power I profess to know nothing further. To me, as yet, it is merely the counterpart of my impotence. I should not venture, for instance, to call this power almighty, since I have no means of knowing how much it can do; but I should not hesitate, if I may coin a word, to call it *omnificent:* it is to me, by definition, the doer of everything that is done. I am not asserting the physical validity of this sense of agency or cause: I am merely feeling the force, the friendliness, the hostility, the unfathomableness of the world. I am expressing an impression; and it may be long before my sense of omnipresent power can be erected, with many qualifications, into a theological theory of the omnipotence of God. But the moral presence of power comes upon a man in the night, in the desert, when he finds himself, as the Arabs say, alone with Allah. It reappears in every acute predicament, in extremities, in the birth of a child, or in the face of death. And as for the unity of this power, that is not involved in its sundry manifestations, but rather in my own solitude; in the unity of this suffering spirit overtaken by all those accidents.[54]

In the last sentence lies implicit the factor that prevents Santayana from moving toward any fully religious position. The God or Matter that is the supreme generative power cannot be the same God whom Christians worship as Love and Goodness. The material creation is too mixed and flawed, too hideously entangled, to allow the attribution of purposeful love and providential meaning to its ways. Hence, though acknowledging our dependence on it for the very possibility of spiritual life, we shall see the fulfilment of that spiritual life as the reward of our own solitude or, as Santayana put it, "in the unity of this suffering spirit overtaken by all those accidents." With those words we come full circle again to the Santayana who, like many an ancient sage or Hindu holy man, found integrity and peace in his own powerful spiritual transcendence. And it is to this likeness that he moulds the figure of Christ, the *Idea* of Christ, as he significantly puts it in the book's title:

This idea of God as spirit, loving the spirit in us and realising in himself all that spirit in us looks to as its supreme good, is evidently *prophetic;* that is, it sees in a vision as an accomplished fact, though hidden from vulgar apprehension, a secret ideal of the heart, and helps to render that ideal clearer and more communicable. Thus the enigmatic presence of God in man signifies the same thing as holiness, or the complete triumph of spirit over the other elements of human nature. And this presence of God, far from destroying those other elements, presupposes them, as it does in Christ, and merely coordinates and purifies them so that they may be perfect instruments and not impediments for the spirit. This is strongly expressed in the inspired notion that Christ, being God, positively chose to assume a human body and a human psyche. Spirit could not otherwise have had a history. The idea of Christ thus represents the intrinsic ideal of spirit; that is to say, the acme of disinterested intelligence and disinterested love.[55]

"A secret ideal of the heart . . . hidden from vulgar apprehension." There stands revealed the Gnostic "illuminé," the godlike being who participates in a divine life through the attentive discipline of his own spirit. For all Santayana's sympathetic intuitions into Catholic Christianity we must not forget the man who wrote in the culminating chapter of *Realms of Being* that the vocation of spirit was "precisely dominion, spiritual dominion, without distraction, responsibility or power."[56] In his own ambiguous and eclectic vein he was an adherent of the spiritual and intellectual triumphalism of Hellenistic and Indian speculation. In that context conversion and repentance, *metanoia,* such as he recounted in the last volume of his autobiography as having taken place in his early manhood, always involved a purified act of the intellect, with the aim of leaving behind the transient fleshly self and identifying with a transcendental self, be it Atman, *purusha,* or Nous. To the Greek philosopher of this type, only the universal form shared in eternal truth; the subjective ego, like everything else shapeless and indefinite, belonged to the realm of the perishable. Divinised through the Nous, however,[57] the wise man becomes, as Santayana put it, "the spectator of all time and existence."[58] There is no suggestion, in this version of *metanoia,* of such repentance in the sphere of the intellect[59] as we find in the biblical tradition and especially in the Letters of St. Paul, where the intellect is part of the flesh and redeemable only by grace and faith.

Santayana managed to identify himself with the Catholic tradition of the Middle Ages only in that aspect where he sensed a prolongation of the calm, speculative gaze which for the Greeks as well as the Indians constituted the redemption and apotheosis of a humanity in the toils of suffering and illusion. Lev Shestov, the Russian-Jewish existentialist, like Kierkegaard close to a tradition of religious thought at the opposite pole to that we have been considering, makes just this point about the Greek heritage of the Catholic Middle Ages. He knew it to be the death-knell of faith:

Greek philosophy, according to Kierkegaard, leads to reason and knowledge, while the Christian philosophy begins where for the former all possibilities are ended, and puts all its hopes in the Absurd. Man no longer seeks to "know" and "understand"; he has become convinced that not only is knowledge impotent to help him but that it will demand that man worship it and see in its impotence something final, calming, mystical even. Kierkegaard returns to faith the position that the Bible had conferred upon it. It is only on the wings of faith that one can fly over all "stone walls" and the "two times two makes four" erected and apotheosized by reason and rational knowledge. Faith does not examine, it does not look around.

The Middle Ages, for which the Greek philosophy was a second "Old Testament" and which believed that Socrates' "know thyself" had fallen from the heavens just like the *Audi Israel,* regarded thought as a looking around. The thought of Abraham, of the prophets and the apostles did not appear sufficient to it but had to be completed and corrected. To tell all, it was not really thought. Of course, this was not openly expressed thus, but everything that could be done was done to bring the structure and content of the truths of the Bible as close as possible to the ideal of the truth which the Greeks had worked out and in which, from the very beginnings of Hellenistic philosophy the Aristotelian assurance, "intellect is a substance completely separated from the soul and is one in all men", was transparent. The Scholastics fought desperately against Aristotle's *intellectus separatus* (remember the polemic of Albertus Magnus and St. Thomas Aquinas against Siger of Brabant!); but even in fighting it they allowed themselves to be seduced by it. The ideal of the "reason that is separated from everything, impassive, and constitutes activity by its very essence" (in the newer German philosophy *Bewusstsein Überhaupt*) responded to the deepest needs of the soul that aspires to knowledge and finds in it calmness and peace.[60]

It so happened that in the 1930s Santayana came across one of the few books of Shestov that had been translated from Russian, *In Job's Balances,* and he wrote to Cory:

> I am now reading a very well-translated book by Lev Shestov entitled *In Job's Balances.* . . . It is modern, mystical, and refreshing: a little Nietzschean, but with a latent belief in the supernatural, in death a great revelation, which perhaps you might like after too much scientific positivism. . . . His (Shestov's) history is weak, and his views of other philosophers out of focus and arbitrary; but I like him for being unworldly or anti-mundane, as apparently Russians are.[61]

Did Santayana quite have the right to that *de-haut-en-bas* connoisseur's tone about Shestov? Certainly he missed, perhaps would not wish to see, the essential point. Whereas Santayana had, like Hegel, tried to incorporate the essence of Christianity into his own quasi-Gnostic type of spirituality, Shestov, from his Judaeo-biblical perspective, like Kierkegaard saw no reconciliation possible between knowledge and faith. Faith in a transcendent personal deity alters the whole aspect of the self; it is no autonomous semi-divine entity, "Alone with the Alone,"[62] but a particular fleshly historical creature whose freedom and fulfilment is achieved in the acceptance of dependence and finitude, not through spiritual dominion. Santayana had an intensely dramatic feeling for the finite, contingent irrationality of existence, but it never led him to seek salvation in the very heart of contingency itself. He sought transcendence, autonomy, and the *ataraxia* of the detached spectator. Kierkegaard considered this to be the sign of a soul in despair:

So the despairing self is constantly building nothing but castles in the air, it fights only in the air. All these experimental virtues make a brilliant showing; for an instant they are enchanting like an oriental poem: such self-control, such firmness, such ataraxia, etc., border almost on the fabulous. Yes, they do to be sure; and also at the bottom of it all there is nothing. The self wants to enjoy the entire satisfaction of making itself into itself, of developing itself, of being itself, it wants to have the honor of this poetical, this masterly plan according to which it has understood itself. And yet in the last resort it is a riddle how it understands itself; just at the instant when it seems to be nearest to having the fabric finished it can arbitrarily resolve the whole thing into nothing.[63]

Kierkegaard's last sentence affords us a hint of how Santayana's religiosity maintained him in a posture that was ambiguous and invulnerable. The causal primacy of Matter, of God if you so wish, Santayana might have added, makes all assertions of religious truth the outcroppings of a power ultimately unamenable to the all-too-human desire for reason and purpose; it can be used to undermine the truth-claims of all creeds and systems, including Santayana's own, to be anything more than the expression of arbitrary and unfathomable predispositions. Yet the frail and fleeting nexus of psychic energies that constitutes a human being can be a divinity to itself by cleaving to the type of good that fulfils its own ambiguously spiritual nature. The intellectual man achieves this through contemplation of the varied operations of the arbitrary power that has generated its own eternal witness. Does this begin to sound rather like A Free Man's Worship? To think so would be to ignore the gulf that separated the temperament of a Russell and a Santayana. The intellectual stance of Russell was Promethean, despite disavowals. The imagination of Santayana revolved gravely and beautifully amid the ancient heaven of traditional spiritual insight and religious rhetoric. But the beauty was tinged with monotony. An essential élan was missing. The gift of self to a personal Providence was missing. Santayana had a theological cast of mind without benefit of deity.

For Santayana, truly spiritual life was characterised by total possession, as when the spirit rests with happy assurance in some datum that fulfils its aspiration toward timeless good. The synoptic glance that articulated all parts of *Realms of Being* would be one such instance of spiritual fulfilment. Hence the air of implacably insulated finality so marked in his mature system of thought, marvellously consoling though its properties are for contemplation. Faith, however—and religious faith is here on a footing with all animal faith—tends toward the not given, the hazardous, the existential; it, too, is a "salutation, not an embrace." For religious experience in this life, as understood by the mystical theologians of the Catholic tradition, this means that "absolute and complete confidence, trust, abandon is what we need." [64] That is far from the self-containedness of San-tayana's attitude to the mystical element of religion. Indeed he would hardly seem to be talking of the same thing:

Tension toward the hidden or distant yields intellectual dominion when it becomes clear intuition; but before being dominion it halts usually at interest, inquiry, or pursuit. And this element of suspense constitutes the transcendent force of true knowledge, which takes the datum of intuition for a sign of something beyond. Such belief involves a claim, as pure intuition does not; it is subject to danger and error, and therefore never puts the cognitive powers of spirit at ease. Spirit instinctively transposes impressions into images, and beliefs into imaginative heirlooms, as in myth and legend, metaphysics and the-ology. To meditate on an article of faith is to replace it as far as possible by an intuition. Imagination advances as material reference recedes, until in mystical ecstacy possession renders all faith unnecessary. [65]

When all due tribute has been paid to the worldly and other-worldly wisdom of the ages so superbly recapitulated in Santayana's writings, it must be concluded that his was an imaginative and aesthetic enterprise rather than a religious one—aesthetic in the high Nietzschean sense, not in any restricted art-worshipping sense. There was also a responsible strain in this courteously conservative nihilist that was lacking in Nietzsche. Perhaps these words of his own, which he quotes at the end of *The Last Puritan*, catch the right note: "After life is over and the world has gone up in smoke, what realities might the spirit in us still call its own without illusion save the form of those very illusions which have made up our story?"

It is to the philosophical novel from which those words come that we must finally turn. *The Last Puritan* is in some ways the most adequate rendering of Santayana's intensely felt vision of existence as form and play, against a background of ambiguously mitigated irrationalism. Yet that book, with the more intimate glimpse of his personality it allows, hints at the shadow of some possibly unresolved conflict to which we must finally pay heed.

Epilogue: *The Last Puritan*

THE impression hitherto gained of Santayana is of a man and thinker who consciously strove to be all of a piece. Scepticism holds other men's views at bay; dogmatism grounds all existence in the fertile chaos of matter; style seals the package with an air of triumphantly serene inevitability. His pessimism is cosmically complete, and apparently comfortable. An anchorite *di lusso,* he gazes down from his well-padded pinnacle of detached disillusion upon all the varied insects self-importantly grubbing around on the earth beneath. Those little swirling vortices of dust are the idealistic glosses—religions, political mythologies, theories of historical progress—that the insects put upon their fated organic strivings. Yet some of the insects may change into butterflies, whose happy flights and flaunting colours cause the indulgent sage to view them with aesthetic delight. Life, when it attains any kind of intrinsic perfection, is a self-justifying phase of matter. It comes from nothing and leads nowhere. Yet its energies, even if rash and blind, can be gloriously self-vindicating when not "sicklied o'er" with too much thought.

Pagan aestheticism, given warrant by Santayana's pleasure in the forms that blind existence may assume, finds its spokesman in *The Last Puritan's* Mario van der Weyer— "Vanny," as he came to be known. At a point near the end of the novel, when the First World War has just broken out, Mario is discussing the prospect with his close friend, Oliver Alden. Oliver is a Hamlet-like figure, and the true hero of the novel. He also is made to embody a great many of Santayana's views, and perhaps more fundamental ones, but he had inherited certain "puritan" traits that prevented his attaining the disenchanted serenity of Santayana himself. Oliver has been voicing the usual agonised quibbles of the intellectual concerning the dubious benefits of conflict when Mario turns upon him in exasperation:

You think it stupid, do you? Your philosophy requires you to find a reason for everything? But do you know why you were born? Do you know what you are living for? Are you sure it's worth while? It just happens. Is anything in this world arranged as anybody would have wished—the mountains and rivers or our own bodies or our own minds? No: but we have to make the best of them as they are. And sometimes it's glorious work. So is war. But it's horrible, you say, and stupid, because very likely at the end you'll be worse off than at the beginning. Yes, very likely; and you might say the same of love-making. Nobody would choose and plan it in cold blood. It's a silly business, a sad business; and I know what I'm talking about. Yet love-making is in the nature of things, like childbirth and death, which are horrible too; and no decent person would have put any of those things into human life, if he had had the say about it. Yet there they are; and where would the human race be without them? So it is with war. The world is always full up with people, hungry people, pushing people, barbarous people: you've got to crush them or be crushed. Suppose you escaped to some desert island or to some mountain top, and refused to touch anything that is actually going on: what would you find to do there? Fiddling? Sitting and finding fault? If you're a man you must be ready to fight every other man and to make love to every pretty woman.[1]

Upon hearing those words, Oliver, who is always open to the mental possibilities unfolded by others, thinks of Homer; and though he knows full well that Mario's youthful vaunting is a long way from being the whole of Homeric wisdom, he still feels that "something great, something ancient and fundamental, lay behind Vanny's slapdash sentiments."[2] Oliver had earlier reflected, when the topic of Homer arose at a party in one of the rich Bostonian households he frequents, that

Homer is merciless, covers up nothing, adds nothing, simply tells you the awful truth. Yet he walks on the sunny-side of the world: it's tragedy in the sunlight, despair at high noon, death in the bloom of youth. And you feel that the sun will keep on shining just the same and that the next morning will be just as beautiful and just as cruel.[3]

In this novel, ideas cast off their formal constraints and become living options to be explored on the lips of highly articulate characters who have, for the most part, just enough fictional veracity to be convincing as live presences. The book contains, as Santayana put it in a letter, "all my experience of human life and character."[4] Through Mario, Santayana is seeking to convey the spirit of a harsh, valiant paganism, of a kind that was obviously congenial to him, though never fully endorsed. Mario, whose youthful vitality embraces the flux of existence with unreflecting exuberance, but who has a Catholic tradition in the background to give ballast to his volatile spirits, is in this novel the recipient of all the official accolades of Santayana's judgement. Mario is the epitome of Latin *sprezzatura,* with all the creative vitality that comes from having been born into a settled tradition of wisdom about this world and the next. There is no reason to think that Mario substantially believes in his Catholic faith, any more than Santayana did; but it gives form and cohesion to the moral life in this world, along with a good dose of disenchantment that prevents one taking this world too seriously.

Oliver by contrast is the pensive, troubled Nordic temperament who had "convinced himself on puritan grounds that it was wrong to be a puritan."[5] The Preface and the Epilogue of the novel take the form of imaginary conversations between Santayana and the mature Mario, both living in Fascist Italy of the late 1920s, looking back with sorrowful affection on their young friend, Oliver, who by then had been killed in the Great War. Santayana remarks at one point, when contrasting Mario's career with the spiritual impasse that Oliver's had reached:

You are all of a piece, and your evolution has been natural. . . . Your modernness sucks in all the sap of the past, like the modernness of the new Italy; and any future worth having will spring from men like you, not from weedy intellectuals or self-inhibited puritans. Fortune will never smile on those who disown the living forces of nature. You can well afford to let an old philosopher here and there anticipate death and live as much as possible in eternity. The truth cannot help triumphing at the last judgement. Perhaps it cannot triumph before. Perhaps, while life lasts, in order to reconcile mankind with reality, fiction in some directions may be more needful than truth. You are at home in the grand tradition. With the beautiful Donna Laura and your charming children, you will hand on the torch of true civilisation; or rather, in this classic Italy, you have little need of tradition and torches. You have blood within and sunlight above, and are true enough to the past in being true to yourselves.[6]

There is unintended irony in such a passage. Fascist Italy, into which the pagan-Catholic Mario fitted so nicely, and which Santayana viewed so indulgently, was heading for a very sticky finish. On the other hand, such worldly defeat was not likely to have much troubled Santayana because, like so many Spaniards of an older generation, he fundamentally despised the world. This was something far deeper in him than any shade or variety of humanism. If things in the world could make a brave show, so much the better—that is what he liked about Mario's career. But over them impends God, or Nada. Gerald Brenan, in *South From Granada*, tells us that in the Spanish village where he lived

the cemetery was known as the *tierra de la verdad*, or place of truth. When I questioned my housekeeper about this, she replied with great feeling: "Why, that's the only truth there is. One is buried and that's the end. All our life is an illusion." Rosario is a cheerful and pagan-minded woman with few cares in the world, yet, when asked, she gave the eternal Spanish answer, "Life is an illusion because it ends."[7]

Santayana lived and wrote very much in the spirit of Brenan's Rosario.

Henry de Montherlant's essay "Chevalerie du Néant" develops a type of nihilistic religiosity based on the visual suggestions of Spanish Plateresque architecture. The passage from it that follows has something of the hauteur to be found in Santayana as in Montherlant. Notwithstanding the restraint, sagacity, and occasional demureness present in Santayana's writings, especially the early ones, there was a dark kernel of spiritual extremism in his temperament; it is this that makes his prose at its greatest such a rich instrument of scornful elevation. What follows by Montherlant would have been much to his taste:

You are familiar with the Plateresque, that first manifestation of Renaissance Spanish architecture. A façade that is not a façade but a wall, arid, a long desert of bricks, yellow, pink, and eaten away by the sun. And upon it, set at great distances one from the other on that adorable nakedness and poverty of matter: a gate, or perhaps an oasis of iron, a window weighed down by its swollen grille, magnified by the mighty shadow which it throws in the harsh sunshine, the whole ensemble magnificently emplumed and surrounded by one or more sculpted coats of arms—those coats of arms whence Castile more than any other nation in the world has extracted the fullest decorative effect. And then again, surrounding it, the wall, the vast burnt nothingness. This could be the exact image of Castile—a vast dead space dotted here and there with a few brutal delights, ravishing like drops of water. Those adjuncts are worldly pride, and that burnt stretch of nothingness is Jesus Christ. The perfection of baseless pride, and the perfection of spiritual nakedness and desolation side by side juxtaposed. The blazonry—courage, which enables one to act; and the stripped wall, intelligence, to despise all enterprise. Idealism, which proclaims service; and realism, which knows that the service is useless.[8]

Montherlant's spiritual impression of Spanish Plateresque accords with the affinity Santayana felt for the Baroque. Baroque splendour is a gesture of extravagance tossed at the infinitude of the divine. The civilisations of grand forms, of magnificent illusions, even of rococo insolence, blend best with Santayana's doctrine. This comes out in the character of Mario, to the disadvantage of the pensive Oliver:

> The gaiety, the merriment of the mellifluous youth, laughing at his own troubles and at all the world, were quite beyond human nature, as Oliver had experienced it: something like a young prince in the *Arabian Nights,* counting as many years as the full moon days, and breathing his irrepressible sentiments in the words of poets: or like the *Cherubino* of Mademoiselle Favart at the opera, panting with suppressed life beneath a demure exterior. Yet nothing could be more manly, and even rakish, than this voluble stripling. If instead of his topper and tails and immaculately fresh white tie he had worn lace ruffles and a cascade of blond curls, the armour of perfect courage could not have glistened more visibly on his breast, or the sword-hilt in his hand. If the boy seemed to Oliver fantastic and over-elaborate, he also seemed somehow alarming and strangely formidable. The bonbon might be charged with dynamite.[9]

Admittedly there is something rather implausible about Mario when taken as a character in a novel written, loosely speaking, in the realistic mode of modern fiction. The elderly

sage, latently homosexual, was obviously a bit infatuated with
his gilded emblem of youth and high spirits, whereas in Oliver's
characterisation we sense the strains beneath the composed surface that Santayana presented to the world. Mario was his
fantastic wish-fulfilling symbol of ebullient worldliness and
manly sportiveness; those were the terms on which the spectacle
of earthly existence was most palatable. Moreover Mario was
not in earnest about life, though quite happy to slip into the role
that fate had put in his way as a Catholic gentleman of fortune
and good family. Even as he embraced life, he winked at you
over his shoulder. Yet he enjoyed the performance, and wasn't it
better, Oliver reflects at one point, to take everything lightly as
Mario did,

who danced through the whole show as if it were a lovely ballet or a
grand opera? If the *beau monde* could dazzle, there must be some
brightness in it, something that it was a natural joy for the eye to look
upon. There would be no sweetness in love, no loveliness in music,
unless the depths of one's being rose to the call and came to life,
perhaps for the first time, in creating that illusion.[10]

The love of life's surface is perhaps the deepest thing in us:
Wilde, a Wilde vastly deepened and purified, often seems close
to us when we read the later Santayana. It is in the extravagant,
festive, or lyrical moments of existence that our life fetches forth
from its depths all that we most truly are. Art causes our natures
to blossom in this way, music most of all. Mario's mother had
been a great opera singer, and while at Harvard he holds forth to
Oliver about music:

What is it to be transported out of oneself? The very same thing, at
least in music, as to get down deep, deep into oneself, down to all one
might have been and might have felt, if all these confounded accidents
hadn't prevented. You must be transported, you must play a part:
there's no art without making believe, without illusion. But you can
fetch all that out of the very depths of yourself. There needn't be
anything insincere or foreign about it. On the contrary, it's just freedom. All you must do is to shake off your crust, your artificial shell,
because it *is* artificial, and is merely cramping and tormenting you into
being what other people expect or what circumstances require. Art
takes you beyond all that, as if you were mad, or a poet, or in love. You
are inspired: and then, if you sing, everybody that hears you is trans-

ported with you. That's when the whole house goes wild and shouts and claps, as if you had let loose a thousand devils, or angels, inside each of those poor johnnies in the gallery. And you have.[11]

Oliver is responsive to these insights, and he caps them with some of his own, but with a significant difference in the concluding sentences:

Why then, do you laugh at me for liking old English songs that have nothing to do with my life at home? Singing isn't talking or doing business. It's more like praying, or as you say, like letting out the inner man that circumstances have suppressed. You live then at a different tempo, in another world. There you find everything developing and coming around perfectly, instead of stumbling along in the dark and never getting anywhere. I like poetical and idealised and formal things just because *they exist,* because they have wholeness, so that you can trace them and retrace them; you can sing them again and again. When I repeat them, I have done something, I have lived through something great. I am no longer merely a section of the common sewer through which anything may flow. But I don't want to play a part, or sing in an opera, or be applauded. Music is too much a part of myself.[12]

Oliver's spirituality is more inward and vulnerable than Mario's. Yet he is more truly a denizen of the "Realm of Spirit" because he is more reflective and less tainted by those laughing compromises with the world that the hedonist has to make. At the same time Oliver's puritan ancestry makes him absolutise his spiritual detachment and give it something of the righteousness of a calling. That of course is self-defeating:

He demanded some absolute and special sanction for his natural preferences: as if any other sanction were needed for love, or were possible, except love itself. Love, without that impossible absolute rightness, seemed to him a bewitchment. All life, unless you share it, is evidently a bewitchment, a groundless circling and circling about some arbitrary perfection, some arbitrary dream of happiness, which there is no antecedent reason for pursuing, and no great likelihood of attaining. Not having the key to this secret—the open secret of natural life—his reflection came to a stand.[13]

Oliver, dissatisfied with the mere contemplation of essences, was in search of a living religion. A vocation was latent in him. His reason, however, had convinced him that living religions, with all their existential commitments, were mythical through and through. Was not this the dilemma of Santayana's life? And do we not have a sense that his rendering of Oliver Alden's character obscurely enacts a personal drama, due to an intense and not quite focussed relation between author and hero? On this well-rounded, highly polished surface of Santayana's *oeuvre* there was a small crack to be seen, a slight but troubling fissure: Oliver Alden.

The "tall, serious, aristocratic-looking youth,"[14] with his "large clear eyes and pale hair"[15]—"our admirably gentle and admirably stern Oliver Alden"[16]—had a troubled heredity. His grandfather, a rack-renting Bostonian landlord, had ground the faces of the poor with a strict puritanical sense of righteous calling, and made a million. He was murdered by a defaulting tenant. He had two sons, Nathanael, the elder, and a much younger, Peter, who was to be Oliver's father. At the beginning of the novel Peter is still Nathanael's ward. Nathanael is a sour, prim bachelor, obsessively neat and methodical, in whom the puritan heritage persists as a loveless sense of duty to what he considers to be his position in the community. All his spontaneity is dead. Though by temperament a lonely man, he is in outlook the social puppet par excellence, taking his own petty concerns and officious strivings as a central concern of the universe at large—something that Santayana, through his own long residence, was convinced most people did in varying degrees in late nineteenth-century America's desert of business dedication, civic self-importance, and self-confirming religiosity. Puritanism, having begun as a doctrine of perfect dependence on other-worldly grace, had become worldliness incarnate—but a turbid, griping worldliness. The zestful, hustling, enterprising, sheerly materialistic energies of modern America Santayana could accept, but not the self-righteous moralism, the bogus idealism, and the genteel culture. He also despised its random antlike busy-ness. A nice anecdote in his autobiography concerns his mother, whom, incidentally, he never much liked, though he respected her intransigent independence. This Spanish lady had kept her austere self-containment throughout all the years in Boston, and she once disconcerted a deputation of American female acquaintances who came to enquire how she managed to get through the time when deprived of the little gratifications of committees, clubs, and good works. She replied, "Well, I'll tell you. In summer I try to keep cool, and in winter I try to keep warm."

That contemptuous put-down appealed to Santayana, just as it might have appealed to the cynically detached Peter, Oliver Alden's father in *The Last Puritan*. After a scapegrace early career involving women, betting, and the manslaughter of the night-watchman of Harvard College Chapel by accidentally felling him with the College Bible, as part of an undergraduate prank, Peter leaves America for a prudent length of time. He takes to the wandering existence of an immensely rich, mildly corrupt, and unfathomably disillusioned spectator of the human scene "with a half-benevolent, half-contemptuous philosophy."[17] "It almost seemed," his puritanical wife at a later stage reflects, "that he had a *debased* side, as if nothing could shock him; his smile was like a surgical instrument, half hidden away, not intended to hurt, yet terrible. He respected nothing; and if he wasn't gross, it was only because he couldn't be."[18] He is fond of boats and spends many hours reclined in a luxury yacht, sailing from one continent to another, sampling the varieties of exotic humanity, with occasional bouts of opium to soothe him when *tedium vitae* supervenes:

> The light was low, but sufficient for eyes coming out of the dark, and the lustre was rendered omnipresent by multiple reflections from lacquered walls and porcelain objects. He lay propped high, very lean and bronzed by habitual exposure to the sun and the sea-air; his bald head and thin hands looked dark and swarthy against the white pillow and the white night-gown on which his long fingers were spread out symmetrically. His eyes, rather than in sleep, seemed closed by a voluntary drooping of the eyelids, as if in order that a deeper life might flow undisturbed; and there was a faint ambiguous smile on his lips, not unlike that of the two Buddhas whose golden shrines decorated the Poop . . . a strange spirit of holiness, as if life could ultimately escape from perpetual dying and become supreme recollection.[19]

Not surprisingly, his health suffers, and he returns at the age of about forty to take a cure in Little Falls near Boston, at the sanatorium of a Dr. Bumstead, renowned for his modern approach to such problems. Peter, rather implausibly, marries

Dr. Bumstead's daughter, Harriet, a masterful but essentially trivial female whom he imagines capable of giving him a bit of the ballast of normality he needs. (This loveless marriage of Peter and Harriet, Santayana told Bruno Lind at the end of his life, "was *emotionally* based on that between my father and mother," though the circumstances were very different. "But the absence of affection all round was the same in both mothers and in both husbands and both sons.")[20]

Harriet, after Peter has married her, proves aggressive, self-centered, utterly convinced of the centrality and rightness of her own opinions, as of the transcendent superiority of her own cultural backwater. Here Santayana avenges himself on a type of New England self-satisfaction that he endured and abominated for over forty years. Edith, the young Bostonian girl whom at a much later stage of the novel Oliver thinks he wants to marry, is a more palatable and discreet version of Harriet. She is better bred, more truly gracious, better educated, a devout Episcopalian as opposed to an amorphous Unitarian; but with the same inflexible self-righteousness and conviction of the centrality of her own views and concerns found in Oliver's mother. What Santayana means by puritanism in this novel is, one slowly realises, something very wide. It had its roots in the Calvinist doctrine of grace, election, and consequent certainty of spiritual superiority; but when the theological basis was diluted or lost there remained a rooted psychological resistance to any sense of chance, contingency, and relativity as fundamental to natural existence. Humility was a virtue unknown in its true sense to the puritan and nonconformist tradition. Its latter-day secularised versions still had the urge to absolutise their preferences, and to dominate circumstances by transcendental will. This is why Oliver, in spite of everything, remains a puritan; hence the title of the book.

From the loveless union of Peter and Harriet Alden—a trivial, aggressive prig and an aging, disillusioned fainéant—the luckless Oliver is born. From an early age he is physically strong and attractive, intelligent and hard-working. He is given every advantage, but no affection, apart from some hugs from Irma, his sentimental German nanny. He enters into the activities of his life at school—as later at Williams College and at Harvard—

with a rather dogged dutifulness. He is not rebellious, yet nothing makes him happy. When Oliver is about sixteen, his father, who after a taste of marriage has gone back to his yacht, decides to take him on a sea voyage to try to perk him up, and get to know him better. At this point Oliver's real education begins. We are now in full *Bildungsroman*.

Oliver's father offers him an education in disillusion. Peter has chosen solitude, since he is one of those in whom, as Santayana remarked of himself in his autobiography, "Nature has let out her secret." The author endows Peter Alden with a good deal of his own needle-eyed cynicism, which avoids cheapness through the addition of resigned charitableness: "A middle-aged man in the press of life couldn't afford to have friends any more. His so-called friends were only such of his enemies as he might hope to use or to govern." Peter adds, however, "that a man willing to be friendless might yet be kind."[21] The strength of Peter's perceptions is vitiated by his mode of life. His sickliness, his dependence on drugs, and his eventual suicide—done, typically, to avoid inconveniencing others—are symptoms of a search for nirvana tainted by moral failure. He has not overcome the world; he has simply found it too unnerving to take on the world in the first place, and his money has enabled him to put it at a safe distance. A bit of Santayana himself is in several of the characters in the novel. We may sense in Peter's characterisation the author's devious awareness of how wealth in his later years had given a silken lining to his disenchanted perceptions. And although Santayana, unlike Peter, had a truly dominative character as well as an intellect that made his disillusion more than mere enervation, he still lacked a certain vitality.

Near the end of his life, in the course of an illuminating series of letters to Robert Lowell, Santayana confessed that he had always needed contact with youthful vitality and unreflecting energy, and that in early manhood he had admired these qualities "in some of my friends, especially in Russell [Bertrand's elder brother] . . . this brought me into contact with a powerful current in nature, the élan vital which excites me without making me envious. I want my pagan and Indian philosophy for myself; but I prefer an impetuous force in others."[22] Santayana had spent a good deal of time in Frank Russell's company in early manhood and had liked and admired him, even though finding him selfish as well as a trifle coarse. They sailed together on Russell's boat on inland rivers of France during what were probably some of the happiest times of Santayana's life. Russell for him was a twentieth-century version of Natural Man: physically dextrous, a good organiser, capable of getting along with all sorts, probably very good company. It was an open secret among Santayana's circle that the character of Jim Darnley in *The Last Puritan* was based on some aspects of Frank Russell; and much of what Frank Russell offered Santayana is offered to Oliver by Jim Darnley—"Lord Jim."

Lord Jim is a young English seaman who runs Peter Alden's yacht for him, doses him with opium when needed, entertains him, and generally looks after him:

An affable young man, broad-shouldered and ruddy-cheeked in a white topped yachting cap cocked very much over one ear. He wore a double-breasted blue coat with brass buttons, most brightly polished, duck trousers freshly ironed, and spotless white shoes. Half a word on this or that seemed to suffice for his father and this florid young man to understand each other perfectly: they spoke in a low voice, briskly; the stranger had an air of smiling confidence, as if to say: I have done this and so, I knew it would be all right; and this assumption seemed to be confirmed at once by a little nod from Peter signifying, Quite right; just what I wanted.[23]

Already we feel that there is something a bit conspiratorial in the relationship of Peter and Lord Jim, as well as something shady about Jim, for all his wholesome manliness. Lord Jim, we learn, had been court-martialled from the regular navy for some sexual prank, and Peter gave him the nickname in ironic memory of Conrad's young sailor, who also once made a fatal slip, though of a different kind. Oliver quickly finds in Jim the directness and vitality that his divided nature craves, an escape from "high-falutin' morbid discussions," "odious intensity about theories": "How reassuring to lean against an honest unpretending comrade and feel the weight and firmness of the friendly body, like a wall of strength. . . . Lord Jim, with his high complexion and thick hair—such an image of youth and soundness and simplicity, where all else was crazy or horrible or helplessly supercilious."[24]

At an early stage of the sea-voyage Jim strips on the sunny deck and dives into the sea for a swim:

> What a chest, and what arms! While in his clothes he looked like any ordinary young man of medium height, only rather broad-shouldered, stripped he resembled, if not a professional strong man, at least a middle-weight prize fighter in tip-top condition, with a deep line down the middle of his chest and back, and every muscle showing under the tight skin. By contrast Oliver felt very slim, rather awkward, and a trifle unsteady on his long colt-like legs and bare feet, unused to the hard contact of a sloping deck, strangely warm in the sun. Was he expected to dive too? [25]

Oliver is also a bit shy about swimming without any covering, but soon they are splashing around happily, and sitting together on a little raft, talking. Early E. M. Forster comes to mind. Is Jim one of those pagan, faunlike chums who release the shrinking intellectual hero from nerves and intellect and baptise him in the healing waters of life? That would be to get Santayana quite wrong. He views natural life with relish and with respect, but not with mystical sentiment. Its energies are harshly ambiguous.

Jim keeps as a mistress the landlady of a riverside pub near the Oxfordshire village where his father is the vicar, for Jim is a gentleman on his paternal side, though the vicar had married beneath himself. Jim is totally amoral, in the most charming and breezy way. It is hinted that he had murdered not only a ship's mate whose behaviour Peter Alden was finding inconvenient but also the first husband of his pub-keeping mistress. Santayana noted in a letter his surprise that "the dangerous side of the book—and it has more than one such—seems to have been overlooked or timidly ignored by critics." [26] The comment reflects Santayana's awareness that his doctrine of the relativity of good to specific natures had disturbing implications. A powerful natural energy like Jim's will pursue its own fulfilment at extreme cost to other conflicting sources of energy that cross its path; this is what comes of reducing morality to biological forcefulness, which is what Santayana tended to do in his later years. Some energies are successful, and then may consolidate themselves in a stable tradition of life, whence all sorts of "rational" virtues may cooperatively and harmoniously flower. But Jim is Santayana's reminder of the latent, inevitable savagery that lurks in a bunch of energies like the human psyche, when thrusting toward their proper integration and fulfilment. "The most radical way of describing my ethics," Santayana remarked in a letter, "is to say that its principle is not Duty but Virtue. It is only when a particular duty is an exercise of *natural* virtue that it can be binding morally."[27]

The appeal of Lord Jim to Santayana as well as to Oliver lay in his exhilarating vital spirits and his frankness. These were his natural virtues. His fecklessness and his casual murderousness Oliver cannot accept. This shows what a puritan he is! Admittedly Santayana goes out of his way to show Jim declining in the course of the book toward the "louche" and the seedy. But is he making a moral judgement, or simply registering regretfully a biological failure of harmony and integration? It is not easy to say. Oliver's temperament, however, cannot sit easily to naturalistic amoralism; nor can he take his ease among glorious and edifying illusions, knowing them to be such, which is what his father advocates and Mario playfully exemplifies. With increasing disillusion Oliver sees the relativistic status of the varied goods that distract the human zoo, but he takes this knowledge upon himself in all its essential desolation. He is the pure victim of truth, rather than its victorious spectator, which is the role Santayana reserved for himself in the novel. Oliver's sentimental German governess, Irma, gifted like so many of the characters with Santayana's own fluent appraisals, enters his bedroom while he is sleeping. She sees him reflected in a mirror, with arms outstretched toward a brass bar above his bed, and momentarily has an image of Christ crucified; but poor Oliver, she adds in the letter she is writing to a friend, will never know an ensuing glory and triumph; his nature will always be smothered, morally confused, "a conscientious suicide."[28]

Some ultimate consecration to goodness and truth seems required by Oliver's desolate perceptions, but the very terms of his relativism prevent him from attaining it. His creator intermittently laments the weakness of his young hero, yet as the novel draws toward its conclusion his unfailing eloquence seems to be conveying through the character a dimension that does not quite chime with his own formal doctrines, but that powerfully exalts his moral imagination. The free form of the novel releases something in Santayana that his philosophical treatises had curbed:

There might be something enviable in Mario's capacity to enjoy life on so many levels and to identify himself with people of so many descriptions. It might be enviable to be interested and excited by realities, even when they were unpleasant or dangerous or horrible. Enviable, thought Oliver, if you wish to be happy: but impossible if you wish to do right, to make yourself and the world better. You are merely encouraging the fools to be fools, the rascals to be rascals, and the prostitutes to be prostitutes. It was all very well to sympathise with nature. You might fall in love with paganism, as Goethe did; but you mustn't condone nature's crimes, you mustn't become a pagan in your heart. That had been Goethe's mistake. In your heart you must remain a platonist or a Christian, as the Vicar remained: not by any sentimental attachment to tradition or any flabbiness of thought, but because it was the very nature of the heart to choose a pure good, and to cleave to it. There was, there couldn't help being, a single supreme allegiance, a dedication to truth, to mercy, to beauty, infinitely to be preferred to this motley experience and this treadmill of bitter amusements. People like Mario weren't looking for the truth or for the best life: they were merely playing the game. In that sense Mario was more American, more modern, than Oliver himself: or rather he was what men of the world had always been, brilliant slaves of their circumstances.[29]

Although that passage can, I suppose, be made coherent with Santayana's materialism and the relativism flowing therefrom, it lingers in the memory as hinting a dedication to absolute values that his formal doctrines cannot convincingly sustain. In this it resembles Proust's words on the death of Bergotte, when the narrator reflects that

there is no reason inherent in the conditions of life on this earth that can make us consider ourselves obliged to do good, to be kind and thoughtful, even to be polite, nor for an atheist artist to consider himself obliged to begin over again a score of times a piece of work the admiration aroused by which will matter little to his worm-eaten body, like the patch of yellow wall painted with so much skill and refinement by an artist destined to be forever unknown and barely identified under the name of Vermeer. All these obligations, which have a sanction in our present life, seem to belong to a different world, a world based on kindness, scrupulousness, self-sacrifice, a world entirely different from this one and which we leave in order to be born on this earth, before perhaps returning there to live once again beneath the sway of those unknown laws which we obeyed because we bore their precepts in our hearts, not knowing whose hand had traced them there.[30]

Proust was as aware as Santayana of the ultimately futile transience of the energies of the natural world in which human life is a self-deceiving episode. Yet those words momentarily cancel some better known traits of his work, as the words of Oliver do that of Santayana. Was he not more like his puritan young hero then he would have conceded?

Santayana indicates in his autobiography that his life was advisedly a turning away from the world, a dedication to live spiritually among the eternal truth of things. Can one be sure that the consecratory emotion in his writings was ever completely satisfied by his philosophical quietus? An oblique self-revelation may lie implicit in the words spoken to Oliver by Edith, the young American girl who, along with Rose Darnley, Jim's sister, stirs his ambiguous affections. Edith, like Rose, rejects his love, since both sense in him the presence of a calling that will always beckon him away from the rough and ready consolations of a natural career in the world:

I almost think you are one of those rare persons called to a solitary life in a special sense. Are you sure you need marry at all? Perhaps you don't even need the Church; because God has other children that are not of this fold. In antiquity and in heathen nations there have been heroic souls; and so in the modern world there may be some not yet called to the visible Church, but needing to live first, as it were, in the wilderness. It seems very sad; it is very mysterious; but possibly if any one of us believers, with the best intentions, tried to guide you, you might be driven away from God, rather than towards him; because God has always revealed himself in nature and history and in the conscience before he revealed himself more clearly and lovingly and miraculously through Christ in the Church. The right way for you may now be a rugged and lonely one: yet we may find in the end, perhaps in another life, our own different ways have brought us together.[31]

Santayana, as if anxious not to let that striking passage reverberate too long in the reader's mind, is quick to follow with a deflating comment: "This charitable sermon left Oliver cold." It is a hasty slap-down. He does not like Edith. Yet the effect seems graceless, and not merely on the part of Oliver. It is as if Santayana cannot allow Oliver, his Mr.-Valiant-For-Truth, to be set at a disadvantage by any other wisdom than his own. Fair enough, one must concede. It is, after all, Santayana's novel.

Oliver himself takes up again the theme of choosing the religious life—what a *Robert Elsmere*-ish novel this is in some ways!—near the very end, in a discussion this time with Rose Darnley, shortly before he leaves England and is killed in the Great War. The formal views expressed here are those we should expect from Santayana. Yet the desolation marking them has to my mind a note of imaginative conviction that goes beyond the insistently merry detachment of Santayana's more public and prominent commentary in the course of the novel:

"I would gladly devote my life to religion, if there were a religion that was true. But Christianity and all the other religions are so childishly false that I wonder how some people can put up with them. I used to ask your father how he could continue to use the language of the Church, while he silently interpreted it in a sense which the Church had never dreamt of. And he would reply by very deep considerations about the symbolism of all thought and language, and even of the images of the senses; how it could not be a literal truth that was proper to ideas, and how they were all nothing but symbols; so that it was legitimate and inevitable to use them figuratively. I granted all this: nevertheless it would remain utterly repulsive and impossible for me to read the Bible stories in Church in an emotional tone, as if they were true, or to preach about Judgement Day and heaven and hell as if they were facts, when I was sure they were nothing but myths and poetic apologues. Your father fully appreciated my difficulty, and said he would have felt it himself, if his education had been different. To him the language of the Church was native; and it still seemed to him that the facts of moral life could not receive a more penetrating or adequate interpretation than that which the Christian fable supplied. But to me, brought up practically without religion, only the images created by science and profane history were native and spontaneous; and I could not honestly use any others. He dissuaded me from becoming a clergyman, even of the most modern stripe. Those were accommodations temporarily inevitable in certain circles; but I was a privileged being, I could stand alone, I could survey the scene impartially; and if that solitude was desolate, it was also ascetic, religious, and an act of worship to the true God. So that, you see, in order to lead a religious life, supposing I am called to it, I must absolutely renounce being a Jesuit or a Franciscan or even a Cowley Father. There is no occasion, then, to give up marriage or money, or such a place as I might fill in the world. If I did so, I should not be living more religiously. I should merely be living without a wife, without means, without a function in the world, and at the same time without a religion."

"You wouldn't be without a function in the world," Rose said in a changed voice that sounded like her father's, "if you could understand the world or even yourself. Can anyone do anything better in this world than to understand the world and perhaps reject it?"

"You are an ascetic without faith."

"Isn't that rather what *you* are?"

"Shouldn't we make a nice pair?"

"Like two drops of cold water," and Rose, smiling, brushed away two drops of rain that had fallen on her hand.[32]

"Like two drops of cold water." The irony is a poignant one. Oliver, for all his unhappy intransigence and isolation, had a loving spirit, and a kind one. And Rose loved him, though she was fearful to show it, since she knew it would lead nowhere. The news of Oliver's death at the front is brought to Rose and her mother by Mario, who, characteristically, even at such a juncture cannot resist a flirtatious appraisal of Rose's possibilities. He reads to her certain verses of Oliver's, found in his pocket when he died, that end with the lines,

> "Our spirits move
> Like snake-weeds writhing in the flood.
> Men marry as their fortunes prove.
> The times have laid on our two hearts
> The pity, not the joy of love".
> She folds her hands and he departs.[33]

Rose resists all display of emotion until Mario has gone. Then the book ends, with a paragraph that redeems the uncertainty of touch Santayana had shown earlier in his handling of the love between Rose and Oliver—"my Oliver," as he liked to call him:

Meantime, at Hawthorne Lodge, Rose had shut herself up again in her own small chamber; but this time, with no indiscreet visitor to overhear her, she didn't restrain her emotions. "Rose, dear, don't cry," said her mother softly, stopping at the door, opening it a little, but not going in; for Mrs. Darnley stood in a certain awe of her daughter, and didn't wish to intrude into her private sorrows. "No need breaking your silly heart over a young man who's dead and gone. Hasn't he left you a pretty penny, and can't you marry somebody else? After all, he was a stranger to us, and no ladies' man. Yet for all that," the old lady mumbled, dropping into a cockney whine, like those poor women who sell matches at the street corners, "he was a *kind gentleman.*"[34]

In 1939, after *The Last Puritan*'s publication and the unexpected amount of success and discussion that followed, Santayana told Cory about a visit he had in Rome from "Trevelyan, an old acquaintance at King's, who said he had found the end of my novel very affecting, that he had been sorry for my young man. Now I myself had cried over the end, especially 'the pity, not the joy of love.'"[35] That admission, unexpected from one reputed to be such a cold fish, confirms a degree of identification between Santayana and his hero. Cory took for granted some such identification; it is interesting that he also saw elements of himself in Mario.[36] Santayana took care, however, whenever confessing an affinity with Oliver, to preserve himself in his chosen role of detached spectator of existence; but he was always pleased when somebody wrote sympathetically about Oliver. To a young man who had written to him just after the book's publication he replied:

That you should not only understand Oliver, but wish to like him, and should see in my picture of him a justification rather than a warning—all this interests and pleases me very much: because I too admire and almost envy Oliver, in spite of people thinking him a failure. Some say he is a failure of mine artistically, others that he is a failure in himself, morally. I venture to think he is neither, even if not in either sense altogether a success. Hamlet was a greater success artistically no doubt; but he was a worse failure morally, because he was not only overwhelmed by the world, but distracted in his own mind; whereas Oliver's *mind* was victorious. . . . In a word, I think he was superior to this world, but not up to his own standard or vocation. To have been perfect and heroic, he ought to have been more independent; but he was tethered, and hadn't the strength and courage to break away completely. He hadn't the intelligence to see what he should break away to.[37]

To another friend he wrote, "My hero dies young, being too good for this world. He is an infinitely clearer-headed and nobler person than Henry Adams, but equally ineffectual." [38] And to William Lyon Phelps he commented,

> Oliver was a spiritual man, incapacitated to be anything else. Now that is a tragic vocation, like the vocation of the poet; it demands sacrifice and devotion to a divine allegiance; but poor Oliver, ready for every sacrifice, had nothing to pin his allegiance to. He was what the rich young man in the Gospel would have been if he had been ready to sell his goods and give to the poor, but then had found no cross to take up and no Jesus to follow.

What did Santayana have that enabled him to gain this superior vantage point to Oliver? In the same letter to Phelps he wrote,

> It is quite simple. I have the Epicurean contentment, which was not far removed from asceticism; and besides I have a spiritual allegiance of my own that hardly requires faith, that is, only a humorous animal faith in nature and history, and no religious faith: and this common-sense world suffices for *intellectual satisfaction,* partly in observing and understanding it, partly in dismissing it as, from the point of view of spirit, a transitory and local accident. Oliver hadn't the intellectual satisfaction, and he hadn't that Epicurean contentment. Hence the vacancy he faced when he had "overcome the world". *Basta.*[39]

The tone of the letter to Phelps is similar to that used to describe his life and opinions in the autobiography: suave, incisive, a trifle remote. Yet Horace Kallen, the American philosopher, called the autobiography "a shield and a deception." [40]

This was confirmed by others in a colloquy on Santayana published in 1959, in which the participants were men who had known him at Harvard and had kept in contact with him when he lived in Italy. Kallen, whose comments were the most memorable in a collection of moderately affectionate anecdotes, took issue at one point with Ernest Nagel. Nagel said that in the autobiography everybody "seemed to be an instrument" [41] for Santayana. "No," Kallen countered; it was rather that

> he had to shut people out; he had to establish his independence and the sovereignty of his soul, so to speak. This "dweller in the eternal". It seemed to me the most pitiful remark that probably had ever come

from him or from any philosopher who was as disillusioned as he, to say, "I live in the eternal", which was in an interview somebody had with him after the war. And my final feeling about him was that he was a lonely and yearning person who had to defend himself against his own emotions, and that he built these structures.[42]

A sympathetic and perceptive observer like Kallen saw something vulnerable and unfulfilled in Santayana—something more like Oliver Alden; different from the triumphantly serene organism depicted by Edmund Wilson; and different from the "one invulnerable man among / Crude captains" whom Wallace Stevens had imagined. Kallen's remark about building those structures is also interesting. It confirms an impression that there was something compensatory and defensive about the elaborate edifice of Santayana's later system of thought. Kallen goes on, "The man had no companions, he talked to himself. He talked to himself with a pen."[43] "The final feeling you got was that here was a man whistling in the dark."[44] Herbert Schneider at a later stage offered the following reminiscence: "After *The Realm of Essence* (the first volume of his *Realms of Being*) appeared one day he was really bubbly—effervescent—and said, 'Well. I've got a toy now, and I like to play with it. At last I've got a system, and I play with my system like a child.'"[45] That comment recaptures the insouciance of Santayana and raises the suspicion that there may have been an element of schmaltz in the more intimate probings of Kallen. Speculations about whether or not Santayana was lonely or unhappy up there in the eternal do seem a bit impertinent. The view was good, and it was quiet.

Let us take him on his own terms, as we find him for instance in a letter written to Peter Viereck. Viereck was one of a number of young men at the end of the Second World War attracted by the reputation of Santayana as a solitary wise man living in a Catholic nursing home in Rome. He sent him a book of his poems, in which the theme of lust was prominent. Santayana obviously found the treatment a bit raw. He replied in terms that with convenient brevity crystallise a good deal of his outlook and character: quiet self-dramatisation of himself in the role of detached sage; a suave snub delivered in passing to virtually the whole of post-romantic modernism and its cult of experience; resigned determination to live as far as possible *sub specie mortis* in the presence of elevated and beautiful forms that cancel the urgency of living. And a pervading impression that this man, in no easy sense likeable, was immensely formidable:

> I suppose nobody except me has time for tranquillity now. Yesterday I spent most of the morning at the requiem mass sung by the choir of the English College and the priests of the Beda in the chapel of this house, at the funeral of an old Scottish priest (a convert) who lived here and often came to see me. It was tranquillity in view of life and death and of all things, for the service might have been Byzantine or Egyptian or pagan of the remotest times. But of course you have no time for such things in the modern experiment; for life has now become an experiment not the old old story that it used to be. Congratulations. It is what you were born to do and you will be great at it.[46]

Abbreviations

Cory	Daniel Cory, *Santayana: The Later Years, A Portrait with Letters* (New York: George Braziller, 1963).
COUS	*Character and Opinion in the United States* (reprint, New York: Doubleday Anchor Books, 1956).
DL	*Dialogues in Limbo* (London: Constable & Co., 1925).
DP	*Dominations and Powers* (London: Constable & Co., 1951).
ICG	*The Idea of Christ in the Gospels* (New York: Charles Scribner's Sons, 1946).
IPR	*Interpretations of Poetry and Religion* (reprint, New York: Charles Scribner's Sons, 1916).
Letters	*The Letters of George Santayana,* ed. Daniel Cory (London: Constable & Co., 1955).
LP	*The Last Puritan* (London: Constable & Co., 1935).
LR	*The Life of Reason, or the Phases of Human Progress* (New York: Charles Scribner's Sons, 1922). These references appear as LR I, LR II, LR III, LR IV, and LR V, since I have used the 1905 five-volume unrevised edition reprinted in 1922. The numbers refer to *Reason in Common Sense* (I); *Reason in Society* (II); *Reason in Religion* (III); *Reason in Art* (IV); *Reason in Science* (V).
OS	*Obiter Scripta, Essays and Reviews,* ed. J. Buchler and B. Schwartz (London: Constable & Co., 1936).
Poems	*Poems by George Santayana,* selected by the author and revised (New York: Charles Scribner's Sons, 1923).
PP	*Persons and Places, Fragments of Autobiography,* ed. William G. Holzberger and Herman J. Saatkamp, Jr., with an Introduction by Richard C. Lyon, critical edition, (Cambridge, Mass., and London: MIT Press, 1986).
PSL	*Platonism and the Spiritual Life,* reprinted in *Winds of Doctrine* (see below).
RB	*Realms of Being* (New York: Charles Scribner's Sons, 1942). This is the one-volume complete edition, with an Introduction added in 1942. Cooper Square reprint. It comprises *The Realm of Essence,* 1928; *The Realm of Matter,* 1930; *The Realm of Truth,* 1937; and *The Realm of Spirit,* 1940.

SAF   *Scepticism and Animal Faith* (London: Constable & Co., 1923).

SB   *The Sense of Beauty* (reprint, New York: Dover, 1955).

Schilpp   *The Philosophy of George Santayana,* ed. P. A. Schilpp, The Library of Living Philosophers (New York: Tudor Publishing Co., 1940).

SE   *Soliloquies in England* (London: Constable & Co., 1922).

TPP   *Three Philosophical Poets* (reprint, New York: Doubleday Anchor Books, 1954).

WD   *Winds of Doctrine* (reprint, New York: Harper Torch Books, 1957).

Notes

Chapter I

1. Santayana told Bruno Lind the basis of this story: "Sometimes when I went walking I didn't care to take all of a cheap edition along, so I'd cut out 32 pages—two sections—and put them in my pocket. On my desk there you'll see a heavy German book on Alexander the Great. I've cut it up because it's too heavy to hold." B. Lind, *Vagabond Scholar* (New York: Bridgehead Books, 1962), 60.

2. Timothy L. Sprigge, *Santayana: An Examination of His Philosophy* (London: Routledge & Kegan Paul, 1974), 43.

3. RB, 156.

4. OS, 206.

5. RB, 646.

6. "The Idler and His Works," *The Saturday Review,* May 15, 1954, 50.

7. RB, 13.

8. Lionel Trilling, "The Smile of Parmenides," *Encounter* (December 1956).

9. SE, 120.

10. Cory, 150.

11. Letter to B. A. G. Fuller, January 1, 1926, Houghton Library Manuscript Collection, bMsAm 1542, Harvard University.

12. Letter to R. S. Barlow, October 19, 1935, Houghton Library Manuscript Collection, bMsAm 1542, Harvard University.

13. Bertrand Russell, *Portraits From Memory* (London: Allen & Unwin, 1958), 92.

14. *The Letters of William James,* ed. H. James, 2 vols. (Boston: The Atlantic Monthly Press, 1920), 2:122.

15. Cory, 41.

16. COUS, 56–57.

17. RB, 811.

18. Plato *Republic* 9.592.

19. Aristotle *Nicomachean Ethics* 1177a.

20. Werner Jaeger, *Early Christianity and Greek Paideia* (Oxford: Oxford University Press, 1962), 10.

21. A. J. Festugière, O.P., *Epicurus and His Gods* (Oxford: Blackwell, 1955), 86. Out of print.

22. Plotinus *The Enneads* (ed. and tr. Stephen McKenna) 4.4.43.

23. *The Renaissance* (London: Macmillan, 1913), 218.

24. Letters, 238–39.

25. Ibid., 88.

26. Cory, 41.

27. Ibid., 208.

28. Ibid., 40.

29. PP, 395.

30. Letters, 110.

31. Letter to R. Lowell, November 27, 1948, Houghton Library Manuscript Collection, bMsAm 1905, Harvard University.

32. Russell, 88–89.

33. PP, 167.

34. Ibid., 287–88.

35. Ibid., 387.

36. RB, 615.

37. Schilpp, 7–8.

38. PP, 380–81.

39. Letters, 341.

40. *The Selected Letters of Bernard Berenson,* ed. A. K. McComb (London: Hutchinson, 1964), 170–72.

41. Letters, 342.

42. Sylvia Sprigge, *Berenson* (London: Allen & Unwin, 1960), 274.

43. Edmund Wilson, *Europe Without Baedeker* (London: Secker & Warburg, 1947), 52.

44. *The New Yorker,* May 2, 1953, 112.

45. PP, 418.

46. Letters, 382.

47. Wilson, 50–51, 54, 53.

48. "Imagination as Value," in *The Necessary Angel: Essays on Reality and the Imagination* (London: Faber & Faber, 1960).

49. *The Collected Poems of Wallace Stevens* (London: Faber & Faber, 1955), 508.

50. Letter of Santayana to A. A. Cohen of February 9, 1948, printed in *Partisan Review* 25 (Fall 1958): 637.

51. Cory, 324–25.

52. SB, 149.

53. *The Life of Reason,* 1 vol., revised by the author in collaboration with Daniel Cory (London: Constable & Co., 1954), vi.

54. Marcus Aurelius *Meditations* 11.12.

55. RB, 605.

Chapter II

1. H. Bergson, *La Pensée et le Mouvant* (Paris: F. Alcan, 1934), 122–23, 130, 131–32.

2. RB, 274–75.

3. OS, 102.

4. RB, 418, 419–20, 424–25.

5. Richard Rorty, *Philosophy and the Mirror of Nature* (Oxford: Blackwell, 1980), 367.

6. Richard Rorty, *Consequences of Pragmatism* (Brighton: Harvester Press, 1982), xxxix.

7. Cf. RB, 485–86: "The truth, then, forms an ideal realm of being impersonal and super-existential. Though everything in the panorama of history be temporal, the panorama itself is dateless: for evidently the sum and system of events cannot be one of them. It cannot occur after anything else or before anything else. Thus the truth about existence differs altogether in ontological quality from existence itself. Life and motion are gone, all scales are equally real, all ages equally present. Intensity, actuality, suffering have become historical. The truth is like the moon, beautiful but dead. On the other hand, the truth is much richer than existence can be at any moment. Not only does it retain the essence of all moments equally, but it contains much that each moment, and even all moments in their inner being, can never contain, since it contains also the systems which these moments form unawares, merely by co-existing and alternating as they do. Truth might be figuratively called the memory of the universe; but it is far more than that, since the destiny of the universe is included in the truth."

8. *Hegel's Philosophy of Nature,* paras. 247–48, tr. M. J. Petry (London and New York: Allen & Unwin, 1970), 206.

9. *Hegel's Logic,* para. 145, tr. W. Wallace (Oxford: Oxford University Press, 1975), 206.

10. *Athens and Jerusalem* (Athens: Ohio University Press, 1966), 167–68.

11. OS, 168.

12. Ibid., 169.

13. *Hegel's Philosophy of Mind,* para. 384, tr. W. Wallace (Oxford: Oxford University Press, 1971), 18.

14. LR I, 42.

15. LR IV, 225.

16. LR V, 3. This was omitted from Santayana's 1952 revision of *The Life of Reason;* it seems that he could not stomach it!

17. TPP, 190.

18. Cory, 34.

19. Ibid., 312.

20. DP, vii.

21. LR I, 220.

22. Ibid., 221.

23. Ibid., 230.

24. LR V, 252–53.

25. LR I, 21.

26. LR II, 66–67.

27. TPP, 142.

28. *The Greek Heritage in Victorian Britain* (New Haven: Yale University Press, 1981), 21.

29. Translated by B. Jowett.

30. WD, 1.

31. Cf. SE, 188: "Liberalism has merely cleared a field in which every soul and every corporate interest may fight with every other for domination. Whoever is victorious in this struggle will make an end of liberalism; and the new order, which will deem itself saved, will have to defend itself in the following age against a new crop of rebels."

32. As for instance in the somewhat inflexible brand of American neo-conservatism promulgated by Russell Kirk in *The Conservative Mind* (Chicago: H. Regnery Co., 1953). Neither Roger Scruton ("The Significance of Common Culture," *Philosophy* [January 1979]) nor S. R. Letwin ("On Conservative Individualism," in *Conservative Essays,* ed. M. Cowling [London: Cassell, 1978]) refers to Santayana; but their subtler minds would probably find some common ground with his. As does M. Le Fanu in *The Salisbury Review* (no. 2 [Winter 1982], "Conservative Thinkers: George Santayana").

33. LR II, 110–11.

34. PP, 284.

35. Cf. the remarkable description of this ideal in Werner Jaeger's *Paideia* (Oxford: Blackwell, 1944), 2:267–68: "Modern readers . . . are too apt to think that the Greek word *philosopher* means *scholar.* The *philosophos* is not a professor, nor indeed any member of the philosophical 'faculty', arrogating that title to himself because of his special branch of knowledge (teknúdrion). Still less is he an 'original thinker'—how *could* there be so many original thinkers in existence at one time as Plato needs for the administration of his Republic? Although, as we shall shortly see, he uses the word to imply a great deal of specialized dialectical training, its root meaning is 'lover of culture', a description of the most highly educated or cultured type of personality. Plato sees the philosopher as a man of great intellectual power, quick apprehension, and real eagerness to learn. He is averse to all petty details; he is always anxious to see things as a whole; he looks down on time and existence from a great height. He does not prize his life, and cares little for external goods. Display is foreign to his character. He is magnanimous in everything, and has considerable charm too. He is 'a friend and kinsman' of truth, justice, courage, and self-control. Such a type, according to Plato, could be produced in reality. It would be the product of early and constant selection, perfect education, and the maturity brought by years. His character of the philosopher does not at all resemble the typical pupil of the sophists. The 'intellectual' who is known for constant criticism of others is greatly disliked by Plato, and is driven out of his temple. His principal emphasis is on harmony between mind and character. Therefore he sums up his philosopher quite simply by calling him *Kalokagathos,* 'a gentleman'."

36. PP, 310–11.

37. LR V, 253.

38. LR III, 213.

39. Karl Barth, *The Epistle to the Romans* (reprint, Oxford: Oxford University Press, 1968), 258.

40. IPR, 174.

41. *Times Literary Supplement,* August 28, 1981, 972.

42. LR IV, 212–13, 217–18.

43. *Scrutiny* 4 (1935–36): 320–28.

44. *A Human Idiom* (London: Chatto & Windus, 1964), 97.
45. *Times Literary Supplement,* April 17, 1969, 401.
46. "Penitent Art" (1922) and "An Aesthetic Soviet" (1927) in *Obiter Scripta.*
47. J. Ashmore, "Santayana's Mistrust of Fine Art," *Journal of Aesthetics and Art Criticism* 14 (1955–56).
48. LR IV, 215.
49. Ibid., 229.
50. SB, 164.
51. "Art and 'Symbolic,'" *The Kenyon Review* 15 (Summer 1953).
52. Alasdair MacIntyre, *After Virtue* (London: Duckworth, 1981), 53.
53. Ibid., 57.
54. Jacques Maritain, *Moral Philosophy* (London: Geoffrey Bles, 1964), 48–49.
55. LR I, 42–43, 238–39.
56. Ibid., 182.
57. Ibid., 170.
58. Hegel, *Nature,* 248.
59. Hegel, *Logic,* 123.
60. SE, 103–5.
61. M. de Unamuno, *The Tragic Sense of Life* (New York: Dover, 1954), 312.
62. Juan de los Angelos *Lucha Espiritual* 1.11.
63. There is a touching series of letters in the Manuscript Collection of the Butler Library at Columbia University, New York, from Santayana's father to his "Jorge." They are mainly about domestic matters, but occasionally reveal an intransigent scepticism and independence of judgement in religious concerns that remind one a bit of Santayana himself. Also, beneath their rather formal manner, one senses an affection that belies a remark by Santayana that the paternal relation was a pretty loveless one. It seems to have been true about his mother.
64. Poems, 15.
65. Letters, 83.
66. William James, *Selected Papers on Philosophy* (London: Dent, 1917), 238–39.
67. OS, 163.
68. COUS, 36–37.
69. Poems, 33.
70. Ibid., 102.
71. Ibid., 103.
72. RB, 326–27.

Chapter III

1. SAF, 132.
2. RB, 337.
3. DP, 297.
4. RB, 350.
5. SE, 221–22.
6. Ibid., 222.

7. RB, 350.
8. Ibid.
9. Ibid., 342.
10. Ibid., 341.
11. SE, 108.
12. RB, 349.
13. SE, 227.
14. DP, 147.
15. PP, 167.
16. Isaiah Berlin, *Concepts and Categories* (Oxford: Oxford University Press, 1980), 11.
17. F. C. Copleston, "Philosophical Knowledge," in *Contemporary British Philosophy, 3rd Series,* ed. H. D. Lewis (London: Allen & Unwin, 1957), 129, 131.
18. F. Waismann, "How I See Philosophy," in *Contemporary British Philosophy,* ed. Lewis, 471, 483.
19. Van Meter Ames, *Proust and Santayana* (New York: Willett, Clark & Co., 1937), 62.
20. D. Macarthy, *Criticism* (London & New York: Putnam, 1932), 17–18.
21. J. Holloway, *The Victorian Sage* (London: Macmillan, 1953), 14.
22. R. B. Perry, *The Thought and Character of William James* (Boston: Little, Brown, 1936), 1:405.
23. Letters, 438.
24. Schilpp, 604–5.
25. "The Idler and His Works," *The Saturday Review,* May 15, 1954, 9.
26. PP, 118, 125, 123.
27. RB, 335.
28. Ibid., 232.
29. Ibid., 187–88.
30. Ibid., 268–69.
31. Ibid., 716.
32. Ibid., 785.
33. Ibid., 288.
34. Ibid., 280.
35. Ibid., 794.
36. SAF, 37–38.
37. Ibid., 185.
38. Ibid., 188.
39. Ibid., 189–90.
40. Ibid., 191.
41. RB, 106–7.
42. Letters, 111.
43. DP, viii–ix.
44. Ibid., 449.
45. Nadezhda Mandelstam, *Hope Against Hope* (Harmondsworth, England: Penguin Books, 1975), 306.
46. "Letters from George Santayana," *American Scholar* 46 (1976–77): 79–80.

47. DP, 320.
48. PP, 546.
49. J. and S. Lachs, eds., *Physical Order and Moral Liberty* (Nashville, Tenn.: Vanderbilt University Press, 1969), 247.
50. Letters, 413, 416, 417.
51. DP, 427.
52. Goethe, *Faust,* part 2, act 2. Translated by Louis McNeice.
53. Letters, 439.
54. C. Isherwood, *Exhumations* (London: Methuen, 1966), 82.
55. "In its simplicity their existence was deeply civilised, not by modern conveniences but by moral tradition. 'It is the custom,' they would explain half apologetically, half proudly to the stranger when any little ceremony or courtesy was mentioned peculiar to the place. If things were not the custom, what reason could there be for doing them? What reason could there be for living, if it were not the custom to live, to suffer, and to die? Frankly, Avila was sad; but for me it was a great relief to hear that things were the custom, and not that they were right or necessary, or that I ought to do them." PP, 108–9.
56. RB, 698.
57. Ibid., 482–83.
58. Ibid., 712–13.
59. Ibid., 706.
60. PP, 133–34.
61. PSL, 281.
62. Ibid., 301.
63. Schilpp, 28–29.
64. SAF, 76.
65. Preface to Iris Origo's *Leopardi* (London: Oxford University Press, 1935), v.
66. RB, 648.
67. Ibid., 156.
68. Plotinus *The Enneads* (ed. and tr. Stephen McKenna) 6.4.14.
69. RB, 172–73.
70. Ibid., 147–49.
71. SAF, 37.
72. I owe this anecdote to James Ballowe, "The Intellectual Traveller: An Essay on George Santayana," *Dalhousie Review* 50 (1970): 165.
73. RB, 746.
74. Ibid., 737.
75. Ibid., 811.
76. Ibid., 824.
77. Ibid., 652.
78. Ibid., 741.
79. Ibid., 647.
80. Ibid., 646.
81. Ibid., 818.
82. As seen, for instance, in his famous section on Whitman in *Interpretations of Poetry and Religion*.

83. Cory, 213–14.
84. RB, 809.
85. SAF, 15.
86. "Spirit, the intelligent unity and the *implicit* Eternal, is itself just the consummation of that internal act by which nullity is nullified and vanity is made vain. . . . The very fact that we know a limitation is evidence that we are beyond it, evidence of our freedom from limitation." Hegel, *Philosophy of Mind,* 386.
"For Spirit that knows itself is, just for the reason that it grasps its own notion, immediate identity with itself; and this, in the distinction that it implies, is the certainty of what is immediate or is sense-consciousness—the beginning from which we started. This process of releasing itself from the form of its self is the highest freedom and security of its knowledge of itself." *The Phenomenology of Mind,* tr. Baillie, 806.
87. Edmund Wilson, *Europe Without Baedeker* (London: Secker & Warburg, 1947), 52.
88. RB, 715.
89. T. S. Eliot, "Little Gidding," in *Four Quartets.*
90. RB, 795.
91. Ibid., 853.
92. Ibid., 799, 801.
93. Ibid., 727.
94. Santayana's annotated copy of the Bergson volume is to be found in the rare books collection of the Butler Library at Columbia University.
95. Letter to Bruno Lind in the early 1950s, Houghton Library Manuscript Collection, bMsAm 1542, Harvard University.
96. Schopenhauer, *The World as Will and Idea,* tr. Haldane and Kemp (London: Routledge & Kegan Paul, 1963), 2:407.
97. Ibid. 3:53–54, 57.
98. RB, 418.
99. A-rational was suggested to me as a better word. Since Santayana himself is free with "irrational," I keep it and qualify where appropriate.
100. Cory, 195.
101. PP, 167.
102. Ibid., 380.
103. *The New Adelphi* 1, no. 4 (1928): 357.
104. *The Life of Reason,* 1 vol., revised by the author in collaboration with Daniel Cory (London: Constable & Co., 1954), Preface.
105. PP, 387–88.

Chapter IV

1. RB, 211.
2. G. J. Larson, *Classical Sāmkhya* (Delhi: Motilal Banarsidass, 1969), 183.
3. RB, 741–72.
4. In M. Grossman, "Santayana as Dramatist and Dialectician: A Critical Esti-

mate Made with the Help of Unpublished Manuscripts," Ph.D. diss., Columbia University, 1960, 179–80.

5. RB, 65.
6. Ibid., 740.
7. DL, 57.
8. Robert Musil, *The Man Without Qualities*, 3 vols. (London: Secker & Warburg, 1954), 2:275.
9. Ibid. 1:181.
10. Ibid. 2:413–14.
11. Paul Valéry, *Oeuvres II*, Bibliothèque de la Pléiade (Paris: Gallimard, 1960), 1508, 1505. Author's translation.
12. RB, 286, 80–81.
13. Ibid., xix.
14. Paul Valéry, *Oeuvres I*, Bibliothèque de la Pléiade (Paris: Gallimard, 1957), 109.
15. PP, 452–53.
16. RB, 667–68.
17. PSL, 245.
18. *Republic* 496.
19. RB, 286.
20. *Theaitetos* 176.
21. OS, 65.
22. Eugène Ionesco, "Past Tense," *Encounter* 31, no. 3 (September 1968): 14.
23. *The Hellenistic Age* (Cambridge: Cambridge University Press, 1923), 99.
24. PP, 428.
25. Plotinus *The Enneads* (ed. and tr. Stephen McKenna) 1.5.6.
26. *The Enneads* 1.5.10.
27. RB, 809.
28. *Timaeus* 92.
29. H.-C. Puech, "La Gnose et le Temps," *Eranos Jahrbuch* (1955).
30. RB, 178.
31. Ibid., 6–7.
32. Ibid., 606.
33. Ibid., 758.
34. Ibid., 785.
35. Ibid., 737.
36. Ibid., 764–65.
37. *The Laws* 803.
38. SE, 142.
39. L. Trilling, "The Smile of Parmenides," *Encounter* (December 1956).
40. PP, 351.
41. Ibid., 156.
42. *New York Review of Books*, May 12, 1983.
43. RB, 854.
44. SE, 139–40.
45. RB, 765.

46. ICG, 51.
47. L. Bouyer, *The Spirituality of the New Testament and the Fathers* (London: Burns & Oates, 1963), 222.
48. S. Neill, *The Interpretation of the New Testament 1861–1961* (London: Oxford University Press, 1966), 180.
49. ICG, 52.
50. Ibid., 17.
51. Ibid., 115.
52. Ibid., 219–20.
53. Ibid., 101–2.
54. OS, 215–16.
55. ICG, 252–53.
56. RB, 811.
57. *Republic* 518.
58. PP, 420.
59. M. B. Foster, *Mystery and Philosophy* (London: SCM Press, 1957), 46.
60. *Athens and Jerusalem* (Athens: Ohio University Press, 1966), 332–33.
61. Cory, 212–13.
62. *The Enneads* 6.9.11.
63. S. Kierkegaard, *The Sickness Unto Death* (London: Humphrey Milford, Oxford University Press, 1944), 111–12.
64. Dom John Chapman, *Spiritual Letters* (London: New Ark Library, 1959), 173.
65. RB, 665.

Epilogue

1. LP, 629–30.
2. Ibid., 631.
3. Ibid., 585.
4. Letter to B. Lind, November 29, 1951, Houghton Library Manuscript Collection, bMsAm 1542, Harvard University.
5. LP, 11.
6. Ibid., 718.
7. G. Brenan, *South From Granada* (London: Hutchinson, 1957), 110.
8. "Chevalerie du Néant," *Essais* (Paris: Gallimard, 1963), 595–96. For help with this translation I am indebted to Professor B. G. Rogers of the University of the Witwatersrand, Johannesburg.
9. LP, 353.
10. Ibid., 377.
11. Ibid., 495.
12. Ibid., 496.
13. Ibid., 387–88.
14. Ibid., 285.
15. Ibid., 172.
16. Ibid., 95.

17. Ibid., 379.

18. Ibid., 88.

19. Ibid., 210–11.

20. Letter to B. Lind, January 29, 1950, Houghton Library Manuscript Collection, bMsAm 1542, Harvard University.

21. LP, 441.

22. Letter to Robert Lowell, January 14, 1949, Houghton Library Manuscript Collection, bMsAm 1905, Harvard University.

23. LP, 175.

24. Ibid., 243–44.

25. Ibid., 190–91.

26. Letter to R. S. Barlow, May 3, 1938, Houghton Library Manuscript Collection, bMsAm 1542, Harvard University.

27. Letter to B. Lind, July 18, 1952, Houghton Library Manuscript Collection, bMsAm 1542, Harvard University.

28. LP, 274.

29. Ibid., 611.

30. *Remembrance of Things Past,* tr. T. Kilmartin (Harmondsworth, England: Penguin Books, 1984), 3:186.

31. LP, 589–90.

32. Ibid., 683–85.

33. Ibid., 708.

34. Ibid., 713.

35. Cory, 209.

36. Ibid., 99.

37. Letter to D. J. Dowd, August 11, 1936, Houghton Library Manuscript Collection, bMsAm 1542, Harvard University.

38. Letter to O. Kyllman, December 1, 1928, Houghton Library Manuscript Collection, fMsAm 1371.4, Harvard University.

39. Letters, 305.

40. *Dialogue on George Santayana,* ed. Corliss Lamont (New York: Horizon Press, 1959), 52.

41. Ibid.

42. Ibid., 52–53.

43. Ibid., 69.

44. Ibid., 50.

45. Ibid., 71.

46. Letters, 378.

Select Bibliography

Books and Dissertations

Ames, Van Meter. *Proust and Santayana*. New York: Willett, Clark & Co., 1937.

Arnett, W. E. *Santayana and the Sense of Beauty*. Bloomington: Indiana University Press, 1957.

Butler, R. *The Mind of Santayana*. Chicago: H. Regnery Co., 1955.

Cory, Daniel. *Santayana: The Later Years*. New York: G. Braziller, 1963.

Duron, Jacques. *La Pensée de George Santayana, I, Santayana en Amérique*. Paris: Librairie Nizet, 1950.

Grossman, M. "Santayana as Dramatist and Dialectician: A Critical Estimate Made with the Help of Unpublished Manuscripts." Ph.D. diss., Columbia University, 1960.

Holloway, John. *The Victorian Sage*. London: Macmillan, 1953.

Howgate, G. W. *George Santayana*. Philadelphia: University of Pennsylvania Press, 1938.

Jonas, Hans. *The Gnostic Religion*. Boston: Beacon Press, 1963.

Kinney, M. C. E., Sister. *A Critique of the Philosophy of George Santayana in the Light of Thomistic Principles*. Washington: Catholic University of America Press, 1942.

Lachs, J., ed. *Animal Faith and Spiritual Life*. New York: Appleton-Century-Crofts, 1967.

Lachs, J. and S., eds. *Physical Order and Moral Liberty*. Nashville, Tenn.: Vanderbilt University Press, 1969.

Lamont, Corliss, ed. *Dialogue on George Santayana*. New York: Horizon Press, 1959.

Larson, G. J. *Classical Sāmkhya*. Delhi: Motilal Banarsidass, 1969.

Lind, Bruno. *Vagabond Scholar*. New York: Bridgehead Books, 1962.

Lobkowicz, N. *Theory and Practice: History of a Concept from Aristotle to Marx*. Notre Dame, Ind.: University of Notre Dame Press, 1963.

MacIntyre, Alasdair. *After Virtue*. London: Duckworth, 1981.

Munitz, M. K. *The Moral Philosophy of Santayana*. New York: Columbia University Press, 1939.

Munson, T. J. *The Essential Wisdom of George Santayana.* New York: Columbia University Press, 1960.

Passmore, J. *The Perfectibility of Man.* New York: Charles Scribner's Sons, 1970.

Pétrement, S. *Le Dualisme dans l'Histoire.* Paris: Gallimard, 1955.

Ramsden, H. *Angel Ganivet's "Idearium Español."* Manchester: Manchester University Press, 1967.

Rorty, Richard. *Philosophy and the Mirror of Nature.* Oxford: Blackwell, 1980.

Schilpp, P. A., ed. *The Philosophy of George Santayana,* The Library of Living Philosophers. New York: Tudor Publishing Co., 1940.

Singer, Irving. *Santayana's Aesthetics.* Cambridge, Mass.: Harvard University Press, 1957.

Sprigge, T. L. *Santayana: An Examination of His Philosophy.* London: Routledge & Kegan Paul, 1974.

Wenkart, H. "Santayana's Philosophy of Mind and Matter." Ph.D. diss., Harvard University, 1970.

Articles

The Southern Journal of Philosophy 10 (Summer 1972) devoted the whole of a very interesting special issue to Santayana.

Aiken, H. D. "Art and 'Symbolic.'" *The Kenyon Review* 15 (Summer 1953).

Ashmore, J. "Santayana's Mistrust of Fine Art." *Journal of Aesthetics and Art Criticism* 14 (1955–56).

———. "Can Santayana's Essence Reach Existence?" *New Scholasticism* 36 (1962).

Auden, W. H. "Through the Collarbone of a Hare." *The New Yorker,* May 2, 1953.

Ballowe, J. "The Last Puritan and the Failure in American Culture." *American Quarterly* (Summer 1966).

———. "The Intellectual Traveller: An Essay on George Santayana." *Dalhousie Review* 50 (1970).

Biddle, G. "Last Talks with Santayana." *The Reporter* 8 (April 28, 1953).

Blanshard, Brand. "Reason and Politics." *The Saturday Review of Literature* 34, no. 1 (1951).

Collingwood, R. G. Review of "The Realm of Essence." *The New Adelphi* 1, no. 4 (1928).

Cory, D. "Some Notes on the Deliberate Philosophy of Santayana." *The Journal of Philosophy* 48, no. 5 (1950).

———. "God or the External World." *The Journal of Philosophy* 51, no. 2 (1954).

Eastman, M. "Philosopher in a Convent." *The American Mercury* 73 (July–December 1951).

———. "Sex and Santayana." *The American Mercury* 74 (January–June 1952).

Evans, L. C. "Santayana and the Greek Sceptics." *The Southern Journal of Philosophy* (Winter 1973).

Faurot, J. H. "The Political Thought of George Santayana." *Western Political Quarterly* 14 (1961).

Goodman, A. "Santayana's Ontology of Realms." *Philosophy and Phenomenological Research* 3 (1942–43).

Goodwin, W. F. "Santayana's Naturalistic Reading of Indian Ontology and Axiology." *Philosophy and Phenomenological Research* 18, no. 2 (1957).

Greenlee, D. "The Incoherence of Santayana's Scepticism." *The Southern Journal of Philosophy* 16, no. 2 (1978).

Harrison, C. T. "Santayana's Literary Psychology." *The Sewanee Review* 61 (1953).

Henderson, T. G. "Santayana Awaiting Death." *The Journal of Philosophy* 50, no. 7 (March 1953).

Kallen, H. M. "The Laughing Philosopher." *The Journal of Philosophy* 61 (1964).

Kerr-Lawson, A. "Santayana's Limited Scepticism." *The Southern Journal of Philosophy* 18, no. 2 (1980).

Krishna, D. "The Active and Contemplative Values." *Philosophy and Phenomenological Research* 29, no. 3 (1969).

Lachs, J. "Santayana's Philosophy of Mind." *The Monist* 48 (1964).

———. "Peirce, Santayana and the Large Facts." *Transactions of the Charles S. Peirce Society* 16, no. 1 (1980).

Lamprecht, S. P. "Santayana Then and Now." *The Journal of Philosophy* 25, no. 20 (1928).

———. "Normal Madness and Political Life." *The Journal of Philosophy* 49, no. 7 (1952).

Leavis, Q. D. "The Last Epicurean." *Scrutiny* 4 (1935–36).

Linehan, John. "Santayana at Home." *The American Scholar* 26 (Winter 1956–57).

Loewenberg, J. "Pre-Analytical and Post-Analytical Data." *The Journal of Philosophy* 24, no. 1 (1927).

Michelsen, J. M. "Santayana's Non-Existent Symbols." *Transactions of the Charles S. Peirce Society* 9, no. 4 (1975).

———. "Santayana's Platonic Nominalism." *Transactions of the Charles S. Peirce Society* 13, no. 3 (1977).

Oakeshott, M. "Philosophical Imagination." *The Spectator,* November 2, 1951.

Olafson, F. A. "Scepticism and Animal Faith." *The Journal of Philosophy* 51, no. 2 (1954).

O'Toole, E. J. "Some Reflections on George Santayana." *Philosophical Studies (Ireland)* 20 (1972).

Otten, D. J. "The Naturalization of Religion in Santayana." *Philosophical Studies (Ireland)* 23 (1975).

Pemartin, J. "Semblanza de George Santayana." *Arbor* (1949).

Randall, J. H. "The Latent Idealism of a Materialist." *The Journal of Philosophy* 28, no. 24 (1931).

Ransom, J. C. "Santayana's Palm Tree." *The New Republic,* October 22, 1930.

Saks, E. "Santayana and Belief." *Transactions of the Charles S. Peirce Society* 13, no. 1 (1977).

Seifert, J. "Is the Existence of Truth Dependent Upon Man?" *The Review of Metaphysics* 35, no. 3 (1982).

Shaughnessy, E. L. "Latter-Day Janus." *Journal of Aesthetics and Art Criticism* 33 (1975).

Shea, W. M. "Santayana on Knowing and Being." *New Scholasticism* 49 (1975).

Singer, B. "Signs of Existence." *The Southern Journal of Philosophy* 16, no. 4 (1978).

Singer, I. "The World of George Santayana." *The Hudson Review* 7 (1954).

Snow, W. "A Last Visit with Santayana." *The American Mercury* 76 (January–June 1953).

Sullivan, C. "Essence and Existence in George Santayana." *The Journal of Philosophy* 51 (1954).

Trilling, L. "The Smile of Parmenides." *Encounter* (December 1956).

Williams, D. C. "Essence and Existence in Santayana." *The Journal of Philosophy* 51, no. 2 (1954).

Yolton, J. "The Psyche as Social Determinant." *The Journal of Philosophy* 49, no. 7 (1952).

Index